Supervising Student Internships in Human Services

Supervising Student Internships in Human Services

Carlton E. Munson, DSW
Editor

The Haworth Press
New York

Supervising Student Internships in Human Services has also been published as *The Clinical Supervisor,* Volume 2, Number 1, Spring 1984.

The Haworth Press, Inc., 28 East 22 Street, New York, NY 10010

Library of Congress Cataloging in Publication Data
Main entry under title:

Supervising student internships in human services.

    "Has also been published as The clinical supervisor, volume 2, number 1, spring 1984"—T.p. verso.
    Includes bibliographies.
    1. Social service—Field work—Study and teaching—Addresses, essays, lectures.
2. Social service—Field work—Study and teaching—United States—Addresses, essays, lectures. 3. Interns—Addresses, essays, lectures. 4. Supervision of social workers—Addresses, essays, lectures. 5. Supervisors—Training of—Addresses, essays, lectures.
I. Munson, Carlton E.
HV11.S865   1984   361.3'2'0715   83-26393
ISBN 0-86656-301-6

Supervising Student Internships in Human Services

The Clinical Supervisor
Volume 2, Number 1

CONTENTS

Supervising
Student Internships
in Human Services

Editor's Comments

In many segments of our society there is renewed concern with quality and competence. The automobile workers' unions have publicly expressed concern about the quality of their products, and various teacher organizations have established committees and task forces to devise methods to assess competence and eliminate incompetence. The helping professions have not been immune from these concerns, but the debate does not seem to have reached the levels it has in other areas. This limited response is ironic in that unlike teachers, when confidence in one of the helping professions is diminished, the public can turn to another professional group for service. For example, psychotherapy is delivered by a constellation of professionals including psychiatry, psychoanalysts, clinical psychologists, clinical sociologists, clinical social workers, psychiatric nurses, marriage and family counselors, and educational counselors. In the competency debate the various elements of the helping professions have much to lose when public confidence and support wane.

Long range, serious efforts to increase competence must originate in training programs. Schools are the gatekeepers of the nature and complexion of professions. For these reasons *The Clinical Supervisor* is devoting this issue to articles dealing with student internships. In professional education, the internship represents a major and significant component of the student's educational program. The clinical supervisor is a source of inspiration, guidance and support, and a role model for the student. It is the supervisor who shapes and molds the techniques, methods, style and theoretical orientation of the student practitioner. There is growing evidence, theoretical and empirical, that supervision is a good "insurance policy" against "burnout," and this positive aspect of supervision also holds for student supervision as stress among student practitioners gives indications of being on the increase.

There are many issues about student supervision that remain to be addressed, especially in this era of educational retrenchment. It is hoped that this special issue of *The Clinical Supervisor* will serve as one small source of information in this important area.

Carlton E. Munson

Learning to Interview:
The Quality of Training Opportunities

Richard P. Barth
Eileen D. Gambrill

ABSTRACT. This study examined social work students' opportunities to learn, practice, and sharpen interviewing skills. Master's students identified opportunities to observe interviewing models and to receive feedback on their own real or practice interviews. Students reported few opportunities to observe or listen to real, videotape, or audiotape models or to receive feedback on their interviews. Students judged interview training that included opportunities to observe effective models and receive feedback as most satisfying. These results indicate that the training of social work students may not include critical components of effective skill development. Reasons for this and possible correctives are discussed.

Developing effective interviewing skills is considered to be important in all areas of interpersonal helping including social work, counseling, psychology, and psychiatry (e.g., Clark & Arkava, 1979; Stewart, Winborn, Johnson, Burks & Engelkes, 1978; Liston, Yager, & Strauss, 1981; Goldfried & Davison, 1976). To date, more is known about university-based or laboratory training programs (e.g., Burian, 1976; Keane, Black, Collins, & Vinson, 1982; Schinke, Blythe, Gilchrist & Smith, 1980) than about programs in other field settings. For example, the amount of opportunity that graduate social work students have to observe interviewing models, practice interviewing skills, and receive performance-based feedback in the field are not known. This study considers supervisors'

Richard Barth is Assistant Professor and Eileen Gambrill is Professor, School of Social Welfare, University of California, Berkeley. The authors thank Lois Holt, Sharon Ikami and Ruth Mundy for skillfully preparing the study questionnaire and this manuscript. Reprints are available on request from Rick Barth, 209 Haviland Hall, School of Social Welfare, University of California, Berkeley, CA 94720.

provision of such crucial ingredients of training (Gagne, 1977) to their student supervisees.

Research is sparse concerning social work students' field interviewing experiences. Only a few studies on student's interview training experiences precede this one. Schubert (1963) found that first-year master's degree students observed skilled models interviewing for only a quarter of an hour, met with supervisors for an hour and one-half, and interviewed clients for an hour and three-quarters in a typical sixteen-hour-per-week field placement. Korbelik and Epstein (1976) compared the interviewing skills of students required to spend the usual 15 hours a week in field supervision with the skills of students released from this requirement and supervised by university faculty who provided feedback on supervisees' audiotaped interviews. Despite a shorter time spent in the field each week, skill levels were higher among students receiving university-based supervision. Further, their study suggests that students in both conditions had few opportunities to practice and master critical interviewing skills, and instead, spent much time in "professional socialization behavior" (meetings, report writing, case conferences) that were found to be unrelated to skill acquisition. These findings suggest that graduate social work students have few chances to observe, practice, or receive feedback on their interviews.

Are students' exposure to direct learning opportunities as limited as these studies suggest? The present study attempts to answer this by identifying the amount and type of interview training that social work supervisors provide to students. Although recognizing that meetings and mutual problem-solving serve important training purposes, we choose to study chances to observe, to be observed, and to gain feedback as key indicators of training quality. Our interest in these aspects of supervision arises from findings that students most easily acquire skills when these are clearly defined, when students observe skilled models in action, when skills are sharpened by practice and when performance is followed by specific feedback and suggestions for improvement (Bandura, 1977; Gagne, 1977; Morton & Kurtz, 1980). This skill-acquisition model is supported by several investigations of how supervisees learn. Mayadas and Duehn (1974) found that modeling and feedback were more effective than process recording for teaching interviewing skills to social work students. Shapiro, Mueller-Lazar, and Witkin (1980) demonstrated that modeling plus role-play training resulted in higher skill levels than role-play practice alone. A comparison of approaches finds that "high-fidelity models"—videotape and role play—consistently produced the greatest increase in interviewing skills (Cormier, Hackney, & Segrist, 1974). In a study by Stone and Stein (1975), modeling followed by role-play practice increased students' actual and self-perceived efficacy with clients. A review of research on practicum supervision concluded that supervisors who model facilitative behavior are more effective than supervisors who do not (Hansen, Pound, & Petro, 1976). Immediate verbal feedback has also been found to be effective in increasing empathic responses (Carlson, 1974).

The present study describes students' exposure to skilled models, practice opportunities, and receipt of feedback on satisfaction with interview training over a two-year MSW program. First and second-year students reported on opportunities to observe a variety of models and to receive feedback from a range of sources on their own interviewing or practice trials.

SAMPLE AND METHOD

The study was conducted in a school of social work in an urban area. At the end of each academic quarter, first and second-year direct-service MSW students anonymously completed questionnaires concerning their interview experiences. Roughly one-half of all direct-service students answered the questionnaire each quarter. A total of 225 questionnaires was gathered across the three quarters. Although the anonymity of responses prevented the tracking of individual students across quarters, 96% and 98% of Fall and Winter respondents reported subsequently filling out questionnaires in the Winter and Spring. Completed questionnaires were greatest in Fall (n = 79) followed by Winter (n = 74) and Spring (n = 72). The inferential statistics, reported later in this paper, include only the Spring data to avoid violating assumptions of independence between quarterly responses from the same student.

First and second-year cohorts did not differ with regard to sex or program concentration at any of the three testing points. Overall, slightly more respondents (54%) were first-year students. Women respondents outnumbered men by 4 to 1 with equal numbers of students specializing in "mental health" and "children and families." Students had a median age of 27 years and more than two years postbaccalaureate practice experience. Students were in field placements two days a week in the first year and three days a week in the seccond. The make-up of the sample closely approximates that of the total master's program.

Students recorded the number of times during the previous quarter that they observed—either in person or on videotape—actual and simulated interviews in their field placements. Students noted whether observed interviews were conducted by supervisors, other staff, or "expert" (well-known local or national figures) interviewers. Students also identified the frequency of feedback from field supervisors based on their own real and role-played, live or recorded interviews. The average amount of time spent each week receiving supervision, interviewing clients, and attending staff meetings was also noted. Students rated their degree of satisfaction with field interview training on a five-point scale ranging from (1) Strongly Disagree, to (5) Strongly Agree.

RESULTS

Supervisors rarely served as a model of interviewing during the entire three quarters. On the average, students observed their supervisor just three times per year (see Table 1). In addition to having few chances to observe supervisors in action, students were rarely exposed to role-played interviews or video or audiotape recordings of supervisor interviews. Little advantage was taken of the burgeoning commercial and professionally-sponsored materials available on audiotape. Opportunities to observe other staff interviewing in person comprised the bulk of students' exposure to skilled models. Exposure to skilled models was also uncommon in the classroom. Students wanted exposure to more models of interviewing. On a scale of (1) to (5) with (5) indicating high desire, students expressed strong wishes to observe more interviewing, whether live ($M = 4.64$, $SD = 10$, on video ($M = 4.65$, $SD = 1.2$), or on audiotape ($M = 4.07$, $SD = .94$).

Supervisors rarely provided feedback based on students' performance during actual interviews with clients. They provided feedback on less than three client interviews per year ($M = 2.74$, $SD = .48$) and observed not even one role-played interview per year ($M = .87$, $SD = .29$). Students' interviews with clients were rarely recorded on audiotape ($M = 1.14$, $SD = .36$) or videotape ($M = .54$, $SD = .17$) recordings. Taped role-played interviews were not used at all. Students received even less feedback

TABLE 1

Frequency of Exposure to Skilled Models

	Supervisor	Staff	Expert	Instructor	Expert
LIVE INTERVIEWS					
Real	3.00^a $(4.80)^b$	4.80 (5.70)	1.20 (5.10)	c ___	c ___
Role-played	1.10 (3.00)	0.15 (1.17)	1.10 (3.30)	2.10 (3.90)	0.60 (2.30)
VIDEOTAPED INTERVIEWS					
Real	0.30 (2.00)	0.90 (3.10)	2.10 (3.90)	0.15 (0.82)	3.30 (4.50)
Role-played	0.00 (-)	0.00 (-)	0.83 (2.70)	1.14 (2.70)	0.99 (2.90)
AUDIOTAPED INTERVIEWS					
Real	0.21 (1.08)	0.54 (0.12)	0.54 (2.20)	0.18 (0.96)	0.54 (2.40)
Role-played	0.12 (1.11)	0.00 (-)	0.00 (-)	0.27 (1.26)	0.21 (0.96)

[a]Mean number of opportunities to observe supervisor interviewing a client per year.

[b]Standard deviation.

[c]Not asked of students

on their interviewing skills from classroom instructors. Feedback on in-class role-plays (M = 1.10, SD, = .29) was, as expected, more common than feedback on audiotapes recorded in the field (M = .08, SD = .01) since few faculty members ever listened to audiotapes or viewed videotapes of students' interviews with clients. Audiotape was almost totally ignored. On five point scales, students expressed great interest in receiving more personalized feedback based either on direct observation of their performances (M = 4.71, SD = .82), or on videotape (M = 4.2, SD = 1.1) or audiotape (M = 4.3, SD = 1.0) recordings.

Exposure to a variety of learning opportunities is strongly related to satisfaction with preparation for professional interviewing (see Table 2). Somewhat surprisingly, opportunities to observe role-played interviews was as strongly associated with satisfaction as observing live interviews. Similarly, supervisors' feedback on simulated interviews, at least as much as feedback on live interviews, had a positive relationship with students' sense of preparedness. Total exposure—the sum of all reported direct learning activities— was significantly related to estimates of interviewing readiness.

Although most differences in interview training experiences between male and female students were statistically nonsignificant, the trends converge to suggest that women and men differ in their desired and actual involvement in direct interviewing experiences. Men had somewhat more total exposures to models and feedback, $t(72) = 1.02$, $p < .20$, and greater satisfaction with field work, $t(72) = 1.12, p < .15$. Male students reported a slightly stronger desire than

TABLE 2

Correlations Between Learning Activities and Satisfaction

With Preparation For Interviewing ($\underline{N}$ = 72)

Form of Training Experience	Field Work Satisfaction
FIELD WORK	
Live or videotaped observation of real interviews[a]	.30**
Live or videotaped observation of role-played interviews[a]	.31**
Supervisor feedback on real interviews	.22*
Supervisor feedback on role-played interviews.	.28**
Audiotape of real and role-played interviews	.20*
Total exposure to field work interview models and feedback	.36***

[a] Includes supervisor, staff and expert models.

*   p $<$ .05

**   p $<$ .01

*** p $<$ .001

female students to be videotaped and to receive feedback on their own performance, $t(72) = 1.31$, p = < .10. Female students sought more opportunities than male students to observe live or video models, $t(72) = 3.46, p = < .001$.

DISCUSSION

Our results extend those of previous studies in describing opportunities offered to students to develop effective interviewing skills. Learning opportunities are sparse. Students essentially teach themselves—as best they can. The authors believe that these findings are representative of the supervision of most social work students. Comparisons with other human services training programs are more difficult to draw. Replication of this study at other social work schools and in other graduate programs would help to clarify the generalizability of these results.

Our findings indicate a strong relationship between students' exposure to skilled models and feedback and their satisfaction and professional preparedness. This finding complements other reports showing that worker satisfaction is related to the quality of feedback provided by supervisors (e.g., Kadushin, 1976). Students' competence in counseling is also related to satisfaction with supervision (Worthington & Roehlke, 1979; Lanning, 1971; Bibbo, 1974). Trial-and-error is a slow, frustrating and ineffective instructor. Boosts to interviewing effectiveness are less likely to result from repeated but solitary practice, or even from supervisors' critical responses to after-the-fact reports of interviews, than from specific feedback based on observation of students' performances. Effective feedback can come from several sources, including peers. Like subjects in previous investigations (e.g., Canfield, Eley, Rollman, & Schur, 1975; Schur, 1979), students in the present study also positively evaluated watching peers perform and receiving feedback from peers. Supervisors would do well to promote such opportunities. Supervisors could also comment on student performance in simulated interviews with considerably greater frequency. Our findings also suggest some unevenness in opportunities provided to male and female students. Supervisors should see that practice opportunities and feedback are provided to all supervisees in equal measure.

The limited opportunity to observe supervisors in action or other skilled workers is disquieting. Students denied access to a variety of models and interview situations lose opportunities to stabilize and broaden their interviewing skills (Zastrow & Navarre, 1979). The many benefits of observation from videotape apply equally to live and audio models:

> The videotape gives a faithful record of the live process with all its predictable drama, sudden insights, confusion, and even dullness and repetitiveness. This is a valuable learning experience for students, since they tend to mythologize treatment as a predictable sequence of events by an idealized all-knowing practitioner. Students gain a more realistic appraisal of practice when they view a videotape in which experienced practitioners fumble, miss obvious cues, and even become defensive at times. The students' capacity to risk and acknowledge mistakes then begins to improve, as does overall learning. (Meltzer, 1977)

Audiotapes were the most neglected of modeling and feedback methods. By unobstrusively capturing inflection, timing, and content, they provide objective samples—undistorted by selective attention or memory—of an interviewer's skill (Kadushin, 1976). Opportunities for students to listen to actual and simulated sessions of crisis intervention, grief counseling, and marital therapy, to name a few, were often overlooked by supervisors. The chance to evaluate and celebrate incremental improvements in performance was also bypassed by the failure to gather samples of early interviewing behavior and to compare these with later interviews (Lechnyr, 1975).

In summary, these findings show that interview training was most satisfying to students when it included opportunities to observe effective models and receive feedback based on the students' own performance. Students report desiring these experiences but finding few of them. Efforts to insure opportunities to observe skilled models and receive performance-based feedback in both field and classwork, should yield dividends in enhanced supervisee satisfaction and performance.

CONCLUSION

Why don't supervisors offer supervisees more skilled models, practice opportunities and performance-based feedback? The remaining paragraphs discuss some possible contributors to the failure to include such components in supervision, especially: time, availability of training materials, service concerns, and supervisor's own experiences as supervisees.

Time may be one reason for supervisors' reluctance to allow students to observe their live interviews with clients, to observe students' interviews, or to listen to tapes of student interviews. Allowing students to observe has little time cost. Time saved in enhancing student skills by providing effective models should more than make up for the time taken to arrange an observation time, obtain client consent and introduce the student to the client. Observing students' interviews is more time consuming. The alternatives save little time, however, and provide less valuable information. Reviewing process notes and case records and listening to descriptions of what the student did, is also time consuming and provides significantly less accurate information than listening to a tape or observing the student interview a client. Indirect reports like process recording (which eat up students' time) are known to be inaccurate (Kadushin, 1976). Even more crucial, comparisons between supervisees' reports and videotapes show the omission of more than half of the themes in an interview and the distortion of others (Liston, Yager & Strauss, 1981). Although some authors argue that distortions are the raw data of supervision (Wallerstein & Ekstein, 1959), supervisors cannot know what is a distortion without access to the real thing.

Another contributor to infrequent direct training opportunities may be the lack of training materials that demonstrate effective practice. Several strategies might combat this shortcoming. One person in an agency could assume responsibility for acquiring audiotape or videotape cassettes of skilled interviewers conducting various types of interviews. The ubiquity of cassette recorders makes the use of audiotapes very feasible. Videotape players can be borrowed. Staff might pool their available cassettes and provide a list for students. In addition to increased used of tapes developed by educational media concerns, agencies can develop their own bank of films and tapes and make a list of these available to all supervisors. After all, field work supervisors and other experienced agency staff should also enhance their skills by continuing to observe skilled models. Agencies may also wish to share their list of available tapes with other agencies and social work schools so that unnecessary duplication of efforts are avoided and costs minimized. Time for listening to audiotapes might be found while driving to meetings, to clients visits, or home. To expedite review, students can take responsibility for advancing tapes to critical incidents in interviews.

Or, supervisors could focus on one phase of the interview—review of between-session accomplishments, for example—and not listen to the remainder of the tape.

Concerns about client discomfort, confidentiality, and interference with treatment may also contribute to reluctance to observe live interviews. Clients may experience some discomfort from observation or taping. Supervisors can ask clients if they would prefer not to be watched; many will have no objection. Discomfort should not be assumed (Gauron & Rawlings, 1973). Reactivity to live observers is also less than expected (Reid, 1978). Clients should have the opportunity to sign releases that identify the purposes of a tape's use. Concerns about confidentiality can be allayed by explaining to clients that the interview or tapes will be viewed for *training purposes only.* All tapes should remain in the supervisor's possession and be loaned only to staff and students who sign confidentiality pledges.

Supervisors may not provide models or feedback to their supervisees because these were not provided to them in their own graduate education. New supervisors learn most of what they know about supervision from their own supervision (Akin & Weil, 1981). Instruction in supervisory techniques is rare and badly needed (Gitterman & Miller, 1977). Supervisors, themselves, frequently believe that they are unprepared for their roles (Kadushin, 1976). Social workers exposed to multiple models and performance-based feedback during their own professional education would have the skills and appreciation for the value of providing modeling and feedback. Supervisors would then be more inclined to use such methods when they become the next generation of supervisors.

Several resources are available for supervisors who would like to begin using more modeling and feedback (Austin, 1981; Brown, Kratochwill, & Bergan, 1982; Goldstein & Sorcher, 1974; Morton & Kurtz, 1980; Gambrill & Stein, in press). According to our findings, a new tradition of providing many models and much direct feedback in supervision will appeal to students. We suspect that supervisors will also appreciate the training opportunities and enhanced skill acquisition that such training provides.

REFERENCES

Akin, G., & Weil, M. The prior question: How do supervisors learn to supervise? *Social Casework,* 1981, *62,* 472-479.

Austin, M.J. *Supervisory management for the human services.* Englewood Cliffs: Prentice Hall, 1981.

Bibbo, M.P. The relationship of supervisor-supervisee personality factors and supervisory relationship. (Doctoral Dissertation, Boston University, 1974). *Dissertation Abstracts International,* 1975, *35,* 500BA.

Brown, D.K., Kratochwill, T.R., & Bergan, J.R. Teaching interviewing skills for problem identification: An analogue study. *Behavioral Assessment,* 1982, *4,* 63-74.

Burian, W.A. The laboratory as an element in social work curriculum design. *Journal of Education For Social Work,* 1976, *12,* 36-43.

Canfield, C.F., Eley, J., Rollman, L.P., & Schur, E.L. A laboratory training model for the development of effective interpersonal communications in social work. *Journal of Education For Social Work,* 1975, *11,* 45-50.

Carlson, K. W. Increasing verbal empathy as a function of feedback and instruction. *Counselor Education and Supervision,* 1974, *13,* 208-213.

Clark, F.W., & Arkava, M.L. (Eds.), *The pursuit of competence in social work.* San Francisco: Jossey-Bass, 1979.

Cormier, L.S., Hackney, H., & Segrist, A.E. Three counselor training models: A comparative study. *Counselor Education and Supervision,* 1974, *24,* 95-104.

Gagne, R.M. *Conditions of learning* (2nd ed.), New York: Holt, Rinehart and Winston, 1977.

Gambrill, E.D., & Stein, T.J. *Supervision: A decision-making framework,* Beverly Hills: Sage, in press.

Gauron, E.G., & Rawlings, E.I. The myth of the fragile patient. *Psychotherapy: Theory, research and practice,* 1973, *10,* 352-353.

Gitterman, A. & Miller, I. Supervisors as educators. In F. Kaslow (Ed.), *Supervision, consultation, and staff training.* San Francisco: Jossey-Bass, 1977.

Goldfried, M.R., & Davison, G.C. *Clinical behavior therapy.* New York: Holt, Reinhart and Winston, 1976.

Goldstein, A.P., & Sorcher, M. *Changing supervisor behavior.* New York: Pergamon, 1974.

Hansen, J.C., Pound, R., & Petro, C. Review of research on practicum supervision. *Counselor Education and Supervision,* 1976, *16,* 107-116.

Kadushin, A. *The social work interview.* New York: Columbia University Press, 1976.

Keane, T.M., Black, J.L., & Collins, F.L., Jr. A skills training program for teaching the behavioral interview. *Behavioral Assessment,* 1982, *4,* 53-62.

Korbelik, J., & Epstein, L. Evaluating time and achievement in a social work practicum. *Teaching for competence in the delivery of direct services.* New York: Council on Social Work Education, 1976.

Lanning, W.L. A study of the relationship between group and individual counseling supervision and three relationship measures. *Journal of Counseling Psychology,* 1971, *18,* 401-406.

Lechnyr, R.J. Clinical evaluation of student effectiveness, *Social Work,* 1975, *20,* 148-249.

Liston, E.H., Yager, J., & Strauss, G.D. Assessment of psychotherapy skills: The problem of interrater agreement. *American Journal of Psychiatry,* 1981, *138,* 1019-1074.

Mayadas, N.S., & Duehn, W.D. The effects of training formats and interpersonal discriminations in the education for clinical social work practice. *Journal of Social Service Research,* 1974, *1,* 208-213.

Meltzer, R. School and agency cooperation using videotape in social work education. *Journal of Education for Social Work,* 1977, *13,* 92.

Morton, T.D., & Kurtz, P.D. Educational supervision: A learning theory approach. *Social Casework,* 1980, *61,* 240-246.

Muslin, H.L., Thurnblad, R.J., & Meschel, G. The fate of the clinical interview: An observational study. *American Journal of Psychiatry,* 1981, *138,* 822-825.

Reid, B. (Ed.), *A social learning approach to family intervention, Vol. II: Observation in home settings.* Eugene, OR: Castalia, 1978.

Schinke, S.P., Blythe, B.J., Gilchrist, L.D., & Smith, T.E. Developing intake interviewing. *Social Work Research and Abstracts,* 1980, *16,* 29-34.

Schubert, M. *Field instruction in social casework: A report of an experiment.* Chicago: University of Chicago Press, 1963.

Schur, E.L. The use of the co-worker approach as a teaching model in graduate student field education. *Journal of Education For Social Work,* 1979, *15,* 72-78.

Shapiro, C.H., Mueller-Lazar, B.J., & Witkin, S.L. Performance-based evaluation: A diagnostic tool for educators. *Social Service Review,* 1980, *54,* 262-272.

Stewart, N.R., Winborn, B.B., Johnson, R.G., Burks, H.M., Jr., & Engelkes, J.R. *Systematic counseling.* Englewood Cliffs: Prentice Hall, 1978.

Stone, G.L., & Stein, M. Effects of simulation on counselor training. *Counselor Education and Supervision,* 1975, *14,* 199-203.

Worthington, E.L., Jr., & Roehlke, H.J. Effective supervision as perceived by beginning counselors-in-training. *Journal of Counseling Psychology,* 1979, *26,* 64-73.

Zastrow, C., & Navarre, R. Using videotaped role playing to assess and develop competence. In Clark, F.W., & Arkava, M.L. (Eds.), *The pursuit of competence in social work.* San Francisco: Jossey-Bass, 1979.

Student Supervision: An Educational Process

Tryna Rotholz
Annette Werk

ABSTRACT. Supervision is an integral part of the educational process for student social workers. Educators and practitioners are becoming more aware of the need to develop improved methods to enhance this learning experience. This paper reports on a study of field instruction undertaken at McGill University in order to identify present methods and make recommendations for change. Particular attention was given to identifying the specific supervisory behaviors most and least valued by students and their supervisors.

The history of supervision in the social work profession has been a long and complex one. Most social workers believe that supervision is essential for professional growth and development.[1] At the same time, professional social workers are moving toward the goal of increased autonomy and are concerned about the maintenance of dependence.[2]

Social work supervision is made up of two main components, the teaching function and the administrative responsibility. While the goal of all supervision is to provide improved service to clients, there is an added dimension to student supervision and training. Student supervisors are responsible for teaching professional role models. Their goal is to create a climate which enhances the learning experience for each student, while focusing on the common elements of basic social work practice. This is done to help the student develop both professional competence and a professional identity.

Tryna Rotholz, MSW, is an Assistant Professor in the School of Social Work, McGill University, 3506 University Street, Montreal H3A 2A7, Quebec. Annette Werk, MSW, is an Assistant Professor, School of Social Work, McGill University.

This task requires specific knowledge and skill and there is very little clear information in the literature about exactly which behaviors are most successful in achieving these goals.

The purpose of this study was to examine the process of supervision as practiced by field instructors at the McGill University School of Social Work and to delineate which supervisory behaviors were most valued by supervisors and their students. The study also investigated whether the preferred behaviors could be grouped according to the concepts of emotional support, cognitive structuring and autonomy giving (Table 1).

A review of the literature indicates that a number of articles on this topic were written before 1970.[3] This was followed by a five to six year gap during which very little research was published in this area. Since 1976, there has been a resurgence of interest in the supervisory process. Questions regarding effective field instruction are now being addressed by both social work educators and field practicum instructors.

Dorothy Pettes[4] has defined supervision as a "unique combination of administrative, teaching and helping functions." Similarly other authors[5] have discussed the educational nature of supervision. A limited survey of the literature also reveals discussion about the impact of different supervisory styles,[6] different models[7] and the influence of the setting on teaching and learning.[8]

Watt and Thomlinson[9] studied the role and place of field instructors in the university in order to identify some of the issues concerning social work manpower. They also pinpointed the devalued role of the field co-ordinator. This highlights an important issue for further investigation, i.e., the value placed on supervision itself and on the field supervisor as a member of the university teaching team.

The research conducted by Sheldon Rose et al.[10] provided us with a conceptual framework for the part of the present study which compared the supervisory behaviors most and least valued by students and supervisors. Rose grouped supervisory behaviors into three categories: cognitive structuring, emotional support, and autonomy giving. He defined cognitive structuring to include these behaviors which provide students with information and other resources necessary to structure and/or clarify the work situation and to facilitate the application of theory to practice. Emotional support refers to those actions which encourage the expression of student attitudes and feelings and reward appropriate performance. Autonomy giving includes those behaviors on the part of the field teacher which facili-

TABLE 1

PERCEPTION SCALE ITEMS

A. Autonomy Giving Items

1. Encourages student to structure own work and function
    independently (STRUCT)

2. Encourages student to solve own problems with clients
    (SOLVE)

3. Encourages student to experiment with original ideas
    (ENCOUR)

4. Encourages student to take responsibility for supervision
    (RESPY)

B. Cognitive Structuring Items

5. Helps student to look at client's individual character-
    istics that affect the treatment process (INDIV)

6. Helps student to take into account the various systems
    which affect the treatment process (SYSTEM)

7. Helps student to translate agency policy into practice
    issues (POLICY)

8. Helps student to make links between practice and theory
    (LINKS)

9. Helps student to develop own learning goals (GOALS)

10. Gives direct suggestions and advice as needed (SUGGEST)

11. Helps student to clarify tasks expected in the field
    placement (TASKS)

12. Helps student to evaluate own practice (EVAL)

C. Emotional Support Items

13. Demonstrates clearly by own behavior how student should
    act with others (DEMONS)

14. Helps student to cope with stressful situations (STRESS)

15. Shows sensitivity to student's feelings (SENSIT)

16. Shows interest and concern in student's progress (INTER)

17. Gives encouragement when student is feeling "down" (DOWN)

18. Gives positive feedback (POSIT)

19. Encourages student to feel free to voice disagreement
    (FEELFR)

tate the student's performance of decision-making activities and enhance his independent functioning (see Table 1).

In this article, Rose hypothesized initially: (1) That the intensity
of the student's criticism of his field instruction experience is, in
part, an inverse function of the level of learning which the student

has attained, i.e., beginning students were expected to be more critical than more advanced students. However, his findings did not support this hypothesis. Instead, the reverse was found to be true. (2) That students would perceive their field instructors as providing less or less adequate cognitive-structure than emotional support or autonomy, i.e., less attention is given to techniques or procedures for structuring the work situation or teaching the student. In this case, they found that students perceived greater discrepancy between actual and ideal supervisory behaviors in the areas of cognitive-structuring than emotional support or autonomy-giving.

The process of supervision has three main objectives: (1) socialization of students to both the agency and its community links; (2) the development of social work skills; (3) the development of professional judgment. Since student supervisors have the dual responsibility of ensuring appropriate service to clients and training students to enter a profession, it is essential that some direction be offered as to the best techniques to use to achieve these goals.

The three year BSW program at McGill has grown rapidly over the past few years and, at present, over 160 students are registered in a field practicum. Since the field training is an integral part of the undergraduate program in years II and III, this has necessitated the use of field teachers from over 40 community agencies, hospitals and other settings as well as McGill's own teaching staff.

This raises questions about the role of the university in providing standards and guidelines. If a standardized level of instruction for all students is desired, both training and structure should be provided for supervisors. In order to achieve this, more information was needed about the act of supervision as perceived by both students and supervisors.

The present study grew out of this concern for identifying the components of supervision and the techniques utilized to transmit knowledge from supervisor to student. A descriptive study of field instruction at the undergraduate level at the McGill School of Social Work was undertaken to provide information about student supervision. The goal was to pinpoint some of the strengths of the current methods to suggest some possible areas of change.

The study focused on creating descriptive data along the following dimensions: supervisory training, rationale for supervision, characteristics of the placements, and the supervisory session itself. A perception scale based on Rose's scale[11] was developed and utilized.

Our own hypotheses regarding the perception scale were as follows:

1. In the earlier part of their training (BSW II) students would value emotional support items highly and autonomy-giving items would be seen as less important.
2. We felt that Rose's results, which indicated that students perceived their supervisors as undervaluing cognitive-structuring items would be borne out in our sample.
3. We anticipated that supervisors would place a higher value on autonomy-giving items than on the other two groupings of behaviors.

METHODOLOGY

A seven page questionnaire was designed containing both multiple choice and open ended items. Our intention was to clarify the characteristics of student supervision by exploring the differential effects of setting, level of student and experience of supervisors, as well as the perceptions held by both supervisors and students as to which behaviors most influence positive learning.

Data were collected by mailing the questionnaire to all McGill field instructors and their students. A total of 82 students and 64 supervisors at all educational levels responded to the questionnaire (Table 2). This included 40 matched pairs of individual supervisors and their students.

TABLE 2

SAMPLE DESCRIPTION

SEX	STUDENTS (n = 82)	SUPERVISORS (n = 64)
Male	14.6% (12)	23.4% (15)
Female	85.4% (70)	76.6% (49)
LEVEL		
U2	40.0% (34)	31.0% (20)
U3	29.0% (24)	31.0% (19)
Sp. BSW	23.0% (19)	33.0% (21)
MSW	6.0% (5)	6.0% (4)

Rose, Lowenstein, and Fellin[12] developed a technique for measuring the perceptions of the field experience using an AID score which compares real and ideal perceptions of supervisory behaviors. The present study does not attempt to measure real and ideal perceptions. Rather, it investigates supervisor and student perceptions of the importance of various supervisory behaviors in social work training. Subjects were asked to select the five most important and the five least important items from the 19 item list (an adaptation of Rose's 25 items). Scores achieved were compared on most valued and least valued behaviors for the total sample of students and supervisors as well as for the 40 matched pairs. The items were grouped in three main categories: autonomy-giving, cognitive-structuring, and emotional support (see Table 1).

The data were analyzed by computer using chi square, cross tabulations and t-tests. For selected questions students' responses were cross tabulated with supervisors' responses. Subscores were calculated for each of the three groupings in the perception scale. Mean subscores were calculated for the student and supervisor groups and the significance of the differences between these groups was tested using t-tests. Chi square values were calculated to test the significance of the resulting relationships.

Description of the Sample

Table 2 shows the distribution of the sample by sex and educational level.

RESULTS

Characteristics of the Supervisory Process

Eighty-two percent (53) of the supervisors reported that they had taken a course on supervision and had been supervising students for 2 years or more; 69% (44) of them also supervised professional workers.

Since supervising students is a voluntary part of one's work, a question was directed to find out why, in this time of cutbacks and pressures, social workers still choose to supervise students. Personal challenge and increased job satisfaction were the major positive variables (64%) while the amount of time and responsibility involved (42.2%) was seen as the dominant negative characteristic.

No respondent indicated that this was a prerequisite to job advancement.

Over 80% of students and supervisors reported that they met regularly for 1 1/2 hours of weekly, individual supervisory sessions and that they had frequent contact between sessions. Eighty-five percent of the students used process records as a method of supervision.

Learning Goals

The literature on supervision emphasizes the need to establish clear, measurable learning goals within the supervisory process.[13] Student and supervisor must spend time together discussing their specific expectations and purpose in order to develop agreed upon learning objectives. This is an essential part of their contract and begins with their first contact. Our results show that 79% of students and supervisors "always" or "frequently" set learning goals. When asked to list these, however, many of the goals were not stated in behavioral and concrete terms, and thus were not measurable. One can infer from this that although there is a recognition of the importance of goal setting for maximum learning, it is a difficult task to achieve. More emphasis clearly needs to be placed on helping supervisors acquire the needed skills to accomplish this task.

Perception Scale

Differences between the perceptions of supervisors and students are reflected in the raw scores on items most and least valued. Since the number of items in each of the three categories in the perception scale are not equal (autonomy 4/19; cognitive 7/19; emotional 8/19), a chi square was calculated comparing the distribution of most and least valued items chosen within each category to the distribution of items available within each category. Students weight each of the groups of behaviors equally. Their choices of most and least important behaviors are distributed in the same proportion as available items ($\chi^2 = .07$, P > .1) for least important; ($\chi^2 = 2.24$, P > .1) for most important. In contrast, supervisors feel that autonomy items are least important ($\chi^2 = 6.29$, P < .05) and that cognitive-structuring items are most important ($\chi^2 = 6.05$, P < .05). Table 3 compares students and supervisors on the relative importance assigned to items comprising the three perception groups.

TABLE 3

Comparisons of Supervisors and Students on
Ranking of Perception Scale Items

Item		Supervisors (N = 64)			Students (N = 82)			Significance
		least valued	unranked	most valued	least valued	unranked	most valued	
Autonomy								
1. STRUCT	No.	14	20	30	5	18	59	
	%	21.9	31.3	46.9	6.1	22.0	72.0	.003
2. SOLVE	No.	31	29	4	21	44	17	
	%	48.4	45.3	6.3	25.6	53.7	20.7	.005
3. ENCOUR	No.	21	35	8	16	41	25	
	%	32.8	54.7	12.5	19.6	50.0	30.5	.03
4. RESPY	No.	13	40	11	35	40	7	
	%	20.3	62.5	17.2	42.7	48.8	8.5	.02
Cognitive								
5. INDIV	No.	6	24	34	17	40	25	
	%	9.4	37.5	53.1	20.7	48.8	30.5	.02
6. SYSTEM	No.	7	29	28	12	42	28	
	%	10.9	45.3	43.8	14.6	51.2	34.1	N.S.
7. POLICY	No.	30	28	6	45	35	2	
	%	46.9	43.8	9.4	54.9	42.7	2.4	N.S.
8. LINKS	No.	6	23	35	26	40	16	
	%	9.4	35.9	54.7	31.7	48.8	19.5	.0001
9. GOALS	No.	11	40	13	9	52	21	
	%	17.2	62.5	20.3	11.0	63.4	25.6	N.S.
10. SUGGEST	No.	9	37	18	19	37	26	
	%	14.1	57.9	28.1	23.2	45.1	31.7	N.S.
11. TASKS	No.	21	36	7	25	43	14	
	%	32.8	56.3	10.9	30.5	52.4	17.1	N.S.
12. EVAL	No.	10	29	25	16	37	29	
	%	15.6	45.3	39.1	19.5	45.1	35.4	N.S.
Emotional								
13. DEMONS	No.	34	25	5	62	16	4	
	%	53.1	39.1	7.8	75.6	19.5	4.9	.02
14. STRESS	No.	3	50	11	15	46	21	
	%	4.7	78.1	17.2	18.3	56.1	25.6	.01
15. SENSIT	No.	5	39	20	6	51	25	
	%	7.8	60.9	31.3	7.3	62.2	30.5	N.S.
16. INTER	No.	4	45	15	4	54	24	
	%	6.3	70.4	23.4	4.9	65.9	29.3	N.S.
17. DOWN	No.	16	43	5	26	47	9	
	%	25.0	67.1	7.8	31.7	57.3	11.0	N.S.
18. POSIT	No.	5	45	14	10	45	27	
	%	7.8	70.3	21.9	12.2	54.9	32.9	N.S.
19. FEELFR	No.	8	41	15	13	48	21	
	%	12.5	64.1	23.4	15.9	58.5	25.6	N.S.

A statistically significant difference was found between the ratings of the 64 supervisors and 82 students on two of the perception groupings. Students valued autonomy-giving items more highly than did their supervisors (P < .01). Supervisors valued cognitive-structuring items significantly higher than did their students (P < .001). There were no significant differences between the ratings given by both groups on the emotional support items. (See Table 4).

The differences between students' and supervisors' perceptions were further examined by comparing the 40 matched supervisor-student pairs. These paired analyses resulted in the same significant differences as for the total sample. Analysis of the scores of the 40 matched-pairs with respect to the educational level of the students, (Year II, Year III) pointed out no significant differences according to student perception. However, supervisor ratings indicated significant differences occurred in the area of cognitive-structuring items. Contrary to our hypothesis, supervisors rated emotional support items more important for higher level students and cognitive-structuring items more important for lower level students (P < .01).

In analyzing the five individual items most valued by students and supervisors, cognitive-structuring items were chosen most frequently. Supervisors chose four of these items while students ranked three cognitive items among the first five. The autonomy item, "encourages student to structure own work and function independently (STRUCT)," was ranked in the top five by both groups. In the five items ranked least important by supervisors and students, the least valued item, "demonstrates clearly by own behavior how student should act with others (DEMONS)" is shared by both groups (53.1% supervisors and 75.6% of students) (Figure 1).

DISCUSSION

The early apprentice model of supervision was based on learning by doing under the close supervision of an experienced social worker.[14] This intense process continued throughout much of their

TABLE 4

Comparison of Mean Scores of Total Sample

FACTOR	STUDENTS (N = 64)	SUPERVISORS (N = 64)	t	p (2-Tail)
Autonomy-giving	2.09	1.90	3.18	.002
Cognitive-Structuring	1.99	2.12	3.53	.001

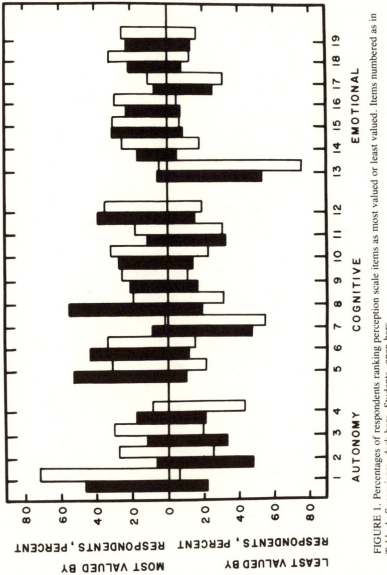

FIGURE 1. Percentages of respondents ranking perception scale items as most valued or least valued. Items numbered as in Table 1. Supervisors, dark bars. Students, open bars.

professional career and workers seldom developed any real professional independence. More recently, a new approach to social work practice based on goal directed supervision[15] has begun to replace the apprentice model. Workers are being encouraged to accept responsibility for their current professional practice and for their future growth and development.[16]

This change is reflected in our results which indicate that students are looking for opportunities to develop into autonomous professionals. They placed significantly greater importance on those items stressing the development of professional autonomy than did their supervisors (P < .01). In particular, the item "encourages student to structure own work and function independently" was rated as most important by 72% of students.

Schools of social work have also begun to refine their attitudes toward supervision as they too have been affected by the new trends in supervisory practice. New information recognizing the unique needs of the adult learner has become available. Malcolm Knowles[17] has stressed both the desire of the adult learner to be self-directing and his developmental need to function in his chosen professional role. Emphasis is being placed on the development of specific skills through the use of live supervision, audio and video equipment. The growth of group supervision in the work place indicates a recognition that mutual sharing and learning is desirable. All this suggests the need for the establishment of clearer guidelines for student supervision in order to maximize the learning potential of social work students.

Our own experience at McGill University has indicated that while students rate the field practicum as one of the most significant aspects of their program, the university does not necessarily place the same value on it. Not only is supervision seen as serving a nurturing function but also as a "housekeeping" task whose intent it is to keep the system moving smoothly. Perhaps this is due in part to the fact that field instruction has tended to be a woman's domain, with its accompanying lower status. At McGill, eighty percent of staff field teachers are women, many of whom are employed on a part-time basis. This in itself raises an interesting dimension for further investigation.

Contrary to our original hypothesis that students would perceive their supervisors as undervaluing cognitive-structuring items, the results suggest that both students and supervisors are aware of the importance of the educational component in student supervision and value a cognitive approach to learning (see Figure 1). Supervisors, in particular, placed a high value on cognitive-structuring items. They recognized that field supervision is a component of the total educational process and stressed the importance of making links between theory and practice. It is important that the universities help them structure the experience in order to maximize the opportunities for teaching and learning.

Supervisors take their responsibilities seriously and see themselves as educators and not as nurturing parents, although they recognize the need to establish a suitable emotional climate in order to allow for maximum learning. It was anticipated that emotional support items would be more highly valued than in fact they were by both groups of respondents. Five out of the seven emotional support items were rated similarly by students and supervisors (see Table 3). The mean response for items in this group was not significantly different. Our results suggest that there has been a shift to goal setting behaviors in both practice and supervision. By setting measurable learning goals, the student and her supervisor can evaluate achievement and the more amorphous emotional support that tended to characterize earlier discussions of supervision may no longer be needed. The establishment of learning objectives tends to create a different emotional climate between supervisor and student. A more flexible and creative form of student supervision may lead to increased mutual respect and greater autonomy.

REFERENCE NOTES

1. Alfred Kadushin, *Supervision in Social Work* (New York: Columbia University Press, 1976).

2. E. Hamlin II, and E. Timberlake, "Peer group supervision for supervisors", *Social Casework,* Vol. 63, No. 2 (February 1982) pp. 82-87.

3. Bertha Reynolds, *Learning and Teaching in the Practice of Social Work* (New York: Farrar, 1942); Dorothy Pettes, *Supervision in Social Work* (London: George Allen and Unwin Ltd., 1967); Sheldon Rose, "Students view their supervision: A scale analysis", *Social Work,* Vol. 10, No. 20, April 1965.

4. Pettes, 1967, *op. cit.*

5. Kadushin, 1976, *op. cit;* Alex Gitterman and Irving Miller, "Supervisors as educators", *Supervision, Consultation, and Staff Training in the Helping Professions,* ed. Kaslow et al., (San Francisco: Jossey-Bass, 1977) pp. 100-114; Thomas D. Martin and David P. Kurts, "Educational supervision: A learning theory approach", *Social Casework,* Vol. 62, No. 4 (April 1981), pp. 240-246.

6. A. Rosenblatt and J.E. Mayer, "Objectionable supervisory styles: Students' views", *Social Work,* Vol. 20, No. 3 (May, 1975), pp. 184-189.

7. Kenneth W. Watson, "Differential supervision", *Social Work,* Vol. 18, No. 6,

(November 1973) pp. 80-88; Marion Wijnberg and Mary Schwartz, "Models of student supervision: The apprentice, growth and role systems models", *Journal of Education for Social Work,* Vol. 13 (Fall 1977), pp. 107-113.

8. Ilse J. Westheimer, *The Practice of Supervision in Social Work: A Guide for Staff Supervision* (London: Wardlock Educational, 1977).

9. Susan Watt and Barbara Thomlinson, *A Study of Trends and Issues in the Field Preparation of Social Work Manpower* (Ottawa: Canadian Association of Schools of Social Work, 1981).

10. Sheldon Rose, Jane Lowenstein, and Phillip Fellin, "Measuring student perception of field instruction", in *Current Patterns in Field Instruction in Graduate Social Education,* ed. Betty L. Jones, N.Y. Council on Social Work Education, 1969, pp. 125-134.

11. Rose, 1969, *op. cit.*

12. Rose, 1969, *op. cit.*

13. Hamlin, 1982, *op. cit.*

14. Wijnberg and Schwartz, 1977, *op. cit.*

15. David St. John, "Goal-directed supervision of social work students in field placement", *Journal of Education for Social Work,* Vol. 11, No. 3 (Fall 1975), pp. 89-94; Morton and Kurtz, 1981, *op. cit.*

16. Hamlin, 1982, *op. cit.*

17. Malcolm Knowles, *The Adult Learner: A Neglected Species,* (Houston, Texas: Gulf Publishing, 1973).

Teaching the Theory and Practice of Student Supervision: A Short-Term Model Based on Principles of Adult Education

Alexander Hersh

Supervision as an indirect social work function has long held an important place in social work education and in the programs of the University of Pennsylvania School of Social Work.[1] Viewed as an integral feature of social work education, courses have been offered to assist field instructors as part of their assumption of first-time responsibility for the field instruction component of the educational experience of master's degree students. These courses traditionally have followed the flow of a year-long, two-semester structure with sessions planned at frequent intervals to correlate supervisory tasks with stages of student development. They have also fulfilled another important organizational need. They have provided field instructors[*] with information about the School's philosophy of social work practice and the thrust of its programs.[2]

In recent years novice supervisors who were recent graduates of the University of Pennsylvania have expressed an interest in having a format which would provide them with concepts of supervision but would not include the already familiar general content about the School's program and ethos which they already know. Additionally, because costs of staff time have risen sharply in recent years, supervisors and agency directors have wanted such courses to be cost-effective. That is to say, supervisory personnel could afford to be away from their offices less. After informally reviewing the needs of this group with the Director of Field Placement and faculty members[**] who had taught earlier versions a short-term structured course

---

[*]The title field instructor and supervisor are used interchangeably throughout. While long an academic issue, it is not a focus in this paper.

[**]Sandra Bauman, Louis Carter and Laura Lee.

29

titled *The Theory and Practice of Student Supervision* was designed based on an adult education.[3] The adult education model was selected when an informal needs assessment suggested its appropriateness. In this paper, factors brought forth in the needs assessment will be reviewed in the context of principles of adult education. The course outline and its rationale are presented and there follows some general discussion to show how the principles blended with a sequencing structure can successfully generate significant learning of the theory and practice of student supervision and provide a substantial foundation for transition to this new professional role and subsequent growth in managing supervisory activities.

Knowles has stated criteria that have an impact on the learning process for adults.[3,4,5] * They are intricately inter-related and profound in the direction they offer the adult educator.

PRINCIPLE 1: TIME PERSPECTIVE AND ORIENTATION TO LEARNING

Unlike child education, which is viewed as preparation for the future, adults are more apt to be interested in learning content for immediate use. Learning in adult education tends to be "problem centered" rather than subject centered. It is a process for problem finding and problem solving and is very much present oriented. To discover what we know and what we need to know are central to adult education. This kind of education is very much a part of one's development since future possibilities become realities as a result of successful present accomplishment.

Discussion

Learning supervisory principles and putting these into immediate use while actually making the transition from practitioner to supervisor is at the heart of this model. The assumption, in fact the expectation is that one learns best by doing and that the richest and most opportune time is when one first encounters the problems inherent in this new undertaking and has the need for specific content for use in this new situation. The new supervisor is assumed, based on her**

---

*Actually the principles are drawn from Ingall's text; they are paraphrased and modified versions.

**The gender term "her" is used because they have been the majority in these courses; "he" will designate the instructor.

behavior to be a self-directed person who has chosen this new role, and wants to succeed. She may be counted upon, therefore, to be strongly motivated and to substantiate the view that "the best time to learn anything is when whatever is to be learned is immediately useful to us" (Watson, in Knowles, pg. 65). In a general sense the problem or task that the new supervisor must deal with is moving from the unknown to the known, from inexperienced to the experienced, from a lack of competency to competent supervisory role performance. The course design has the general problems broken down (sequenced) into stage-related tasks, such as preparing and beginning the relationship with the student, teaching concepts for practice, deepening and sustaining the relationship, evaluating, and terminating the relationship. Within these general guides or milestones the supervisor discovers through experience the specific nature of her own supervisory style and the problems to be solved in order to effectively implement the supervisory role.

The above-described sequencing parameters are further elaborated by written assignments which ask the supervisors to identify, delineate and probe further particular issues that they are encountering and which have a special meaning to them. These then become potential/actual bases for pooling or resource-sharing, and group problem resolution of common elements which are encountered.

PRINCIPLE 2: SELF-CONCEPT OF THE LEARNER

As one moves toward adulthood the self-concept changes from dependency to autonomy. Adults, therefore resent being placed into situations that violate their self-concept of maturity such as being treated with lack of respect, being talked down to, being judged, and otherwise being treated like children. Adults are capable of self-direction in learning as they are in other activities of their lives, they are motivated to learn, and prefer to function with initiative.

Discussion

The graduate of a school of social work who returns to her alma mater, the site of a significant period of learning, faces a number of interesting developmental tasks, including dealing with a changing identity, and an attempt to demonstrate and establish to one's self and one's esteemed teachers and adult role models a basis of new competency. Some uncertainty and anxiety are inherent in such a role transition because one seeks approval while undergoing and possibly completing a process of psychological and occupational separation from the adult (meaning older and more experienced) teachers who have taught one earlier in life at a period of greater dependency.

The act of asking (or agreeing) to supervise a student for the first time is an act of courage and self-affirmation because it signals to the world a readiness to risk, a projection of need and urge to grow, a belief in one's self-maturity and a readiness to be tested on a new and highly acclaimed level (in our society, the terms "supervisor" and "teacher" have a particular status, and position of authority). Given this thrust, it is small wonder that many graduates felt belittled by a course whose structure seemed to signal a disbelief in all of what was going on inside of them. Some suggested that the School had a need to infantilize them, that is, to keep them small, powerless and out of control. Some said that the structure maintained the School's control over them as well as their students and denied recognition of their adult status. They felt pre-judged and believed that there was insufficient recognition of their initiative and motivation as learners. While these inferences sound belligerent, they were not really. The comments relate perceptions, not intentions, possibly some ambivalence about being students again, as well as resistance to having their lives even partially under the control of the School, which may have loomed large as an "authority" force at a point in their lives when they were more vulnerable. It is in fact the field placement director's sensitivity to the need for change and the School's courage to responsively experiment that should be emphasized here.

The notion of self-concept stated in adult education terms, i.e., of a continuum from child (pedagogy) to adult (andragogy) probably does not do justice to the full meaning of a self-concept of "professional" as is the case in an upward-striving profession such as social work. The social work socialization process emphasized values, ethics, and a range of admired traits thought to be congruent with the profession's strivings (e.g., 8). For these reasons, the increase in self-directedness which is symbolized in the social transition from worker to supervisor is urgent. It signifies that one is sufficiently self-directed to be able to direct others! While this may sound contradictory, it is not. It clearly infers the difference between being a learner and being a teacher, between being engaged in a process of mastering and having actually mastered. This is especially important because one's organizational peers and one's own supervisors make this determination and the School quite naturally accepts field instruction agency decisions about persons ready to supervise students. It is, as many novice supervisors have identified, an elegant moment in one's development when one feels deeply within that one now has a *need* to give in return for all that one has previously gotten. Some, interestingly enough have even equated this with being ready to conceive a child. If this is the case, that is, if the existential meaning of professional self-concept is so deeply significant, it is small wonder that the supervisor's investment in having a "first student" is so great, their identification with the young learner so strong and their motivation so splendid!

PRINCIPLE 3: UTILIZING THE LEARNER'S EXPERIENCE

Unlike children who have limited experience, adults have accumulated a variety of different kinds of experiences. These experiences must be recognized and honored as rich resources upon which to draw. Failure to positively use the experience reduces learning potential and may lead to feelings of devaluation, and even rejection of the supervisors as people. Adult education is more often than child education experientially-oriented: adults are teachers as much as learners, and openness to interaction and alternative answers is stressed.

Discussion

As professional persons (usually in their late twenties and early thirties) gain experience and skill in service provision and demonstrate to their employers that they are responsible and talented enough to move up in an agency hierarchy, student supervision is often used as a step upward. The growth that comes from successful practice, and the restlessness that may stem from repetition are often served by this timely move. Novice supervisors seem to be saying that they honor their own experience and the next step can serve as confirmation of professional direction and investment. While we may be accustomed to noting ambivalence in any major move upward an inherent point to be seen here is that risking new growth and the possibility of failure is rather firmly rooted in experience, especially successful experience. The new supervisor is saying by her actions that her experience has been substantive enough, and her mastery of it sufficiently internalized that she is ready to expose herself to a new level and a new dimension of professional performance. Since any new experience represents, in its ultimate sense, unknown terrain, the dual feelings of fear of failure and excitement at the prospect of success may well be universal and therefore normative responses. Beyond that and more importantly, these feelings may serve as a basis for supervisors to establish feelings of identification with their students. They are, in some ways, in similar growth passages—each striving for a new level of functioning and deal with these feelings which are a basis for establishing connection in relationship, yet maintaining a degree of necessary professional separation so that the supervisory can be carried effectively. A major task of the classroom instructor which will be dealt with in another section is how to help field instructors provide supervision emphasizing the educational function.

The symbol of authentic recognition of the rich experience that the supervisor brings to her new task is the point that she doesn't need an abundance of hours of instruction from the instructor, ergo the *Short-Term Model*. To say to a supervisor, "you're experienced, you know the helping process, you only need a few hours of tutoring and exchange with your peers to be able to transfer and apply what you know to this new role—you can handle it," are all honest appreciative gestures which serve as the framework (structure) for a new, adult relationship between the instructor (school) and the novice supervisor. It has many of the strong elements of the contract which has come to be so useful in social work practice.

PRINCIPLE 4: READINESS TO LEARN

A common assumption made by educators is that they must take full responsibility for designing the curriculum of learners. But adult learning needs, more than children's are directly associated with their social and professional roles. In addition, adults are aware of their "problem situation" and their "developmental needs." They can identify their own learning needs and can, therefore contribute to designing their own learning experiences. At transitional points in life the learner wishes to learn what is necessary in order to competently perform certain tasks. She is apt, therefore, to learn what is necessary in order to perform competently. She is also apt to be very receptive to new learning at times when she is most interested in receiving it. These times have come to be known by educators as "readiness to learn" and the "teachable moment."

Discussion

The assumption of a new role such as that of supervision calls out familiar stresses associated with change and the need for coping and adaptational responses. Having established that the practitioner is already experienced and knowledgeable enough to assume this new task, she is, nevertheless, in need of some different theory which can be used to guide, expand, and deepen understanding of experience and provide pathways in the support of her new role. In addition, of course, support relationships, of which the instructor is one, help to stem anxiety associated with exposure and new responsibilities of self. In fact, the anxiety level, strong desire to succeed and the traditionally-held value social workers place on conscientious effort all seem to culminate in a very high plane of readiness and the so-called "teachable moment." The supervisors are eager for direction and they seize upon the experience of learning with relatively few of the typically-known barriers and resistances.* In these courses, the students who have not fit this description have been few. In some instances they either have not been aware of the structured yet intense requirements of the course, or they have not had organizational support particularly in reference to the time needed to be away from their office. For some, the resistance they may bring to this experience seems related to some ambivalence they may feel toward the School—for whatever that relationship may have held in past learning experiences. While such conflicts are not ignored, and are in fact openly discussed, the new chapter of the relationship to the school is stressed. There is a critical rationale for doing so. The supervisor, if she is to be effective, must be willing to identify with the school in sufficient harmony with its thrust to be able to represent it, and she must be able to work in close tandem with the academic adviser. If negative feelings toward the school persist and cannot be managed, the supervisor will be easily split

---

*Some resistance to the course, as may be expected comes in the form of ambivalence about sharing and exposing one's work in monthly papers. Yet, the validity of having them experience this part of the learning may be seen in the general affirmation about papers at the conclusion of the course.

from the school by a student who has a need to use the lack of unity, thus the rich learning opportunities for the student will be lost. It is no exaggeration to say that the essence of the combined teaching-learning relationships come together around this very point because they involve trust in its most significant sense.

The course structure-content design is important, as it provides the learner with a sequencing of learning that past experience suggests most follow (in a general sense). However, there is ample space for supervisors to identify their particular need, design both their own and their students learning activities, and to gauge their own learning to the changes in social and professional roles—as they see them. Resolving problems in their own teaching situation, that is with their own students as they move through this first-time experience is vital to their confidence and is assumed to be their own responsibility rather than the instructor's. But they are given much help and support from the instructor, the student's advisor, and perhaps most significantly from their peers in the class who share in this highly "teachable moment."

We now move to a discussion of the course outline, its rationale as a starting point, and how these priniciples of adult education blend with the sequencing structure to generate learning and a supportive transition to the new role.

COURSE OUTLINE

Session 1: Becoming a Supervisor

Part A: *Orientation to supervision.*

— Preparing the agency for the student.
— Preparing the student for the agency.
— Assessing student level and need; planning assignments and workload.
— Setting educational objectives.

Part B: *Orientation to School philosophy and curriculum and curriculum and student learning.*

The School's goals, thrusts, policies and decision-making procedures; terminology and special concepts, communication between school and agency, expectations and evaluations.

Part C: *Principles of supervision.*

Purposes of a supervision; models and current views. How to begin with a student learner.

Session 2: Beginning with a Student

Discussion of common issues and problems in beginning a supervisory relationship; dealing with conflict and negative aspects of supervisory relationship; engagement as a learner; various "differences" e.g., age, sex, race, etc., in supervision.

Session 3: Deepening and Sustaining Supervisory Relationship

An examination of expectations of the School for student learning; teaching the application of important social work concepts in practice; developing comfort, conviction and effectiveness in the supervisory role; socialization into the profession through teaching values and ethics; identifying the student learning style and manner; developing resources and assignments for expanded learning.

Session 4: Evaluating Student Performance; Setting Goals for Next Term

Review of evaluation process as a valuable approach to development of professional effectiveness and autonomy. Preparation for beginning the next term.

Session 5: Ending with a Student; Further Exchange and Direction in Supervision.

Review of the particular characteristics of the ending phase; helping students to end with supervisor, agency and clients. Review of experience of supervising for the first time; goals for one's own continued growth and learning as a supervisor.

Reading assignments are made regularly (see 6,7).

The course outline shown here provides a sequencing of content and focus based on prior understanding of the student learning process first described by Robinson and then further elaborated upon by others, e.g., Kadushin, Munson.[6,7] The assumption is that a stage-like developmental sequence is useful as a format for the teaching-learning experience. It is a general sequence using time (semesters) as structure, but it in fact supports supervisors to diagnose their own learning need, gauge their own development and evaluate their own learning against the experience of their peers in the seminar. By discovering their own individual expression and style of learning they can use the sequencing as a structure for guiding their skill-building throughout the various stages, with close attention to the need for competency in understanding and mastering the "basics" of supervision. While the sequencing may seem to "hold back" the fast learner, it is actually useful for holding her to the stages of development of the student, and possibly her own assimilation of competency in a step-by-step fashion.

Session 1

After introductions, brief exchanges about agencies assignments, experience since graduation, etc., the instructor presents an overview of the course and his expectations. The need for total attendance is stressed, and each session and the requirements for monthly readings and papers, format, etc., are reviewed with the understanding that this is an outline subject to their input. This approach provides a good opportunity for some facilitating discussion to take place. Here too, the beginning of a sense of group purpose is shaped, and a comfortable learning environment created.

By this point in their professional experience many people have had prior intensive, day-long types of experiences. But the introduction of the format and the indication that, while intensive, the course will be short-term and over by the end of the first semester is both reassuring and anxiety-provoking to supervisors. It heightens and challenges the experience of being adult learners in which they must quickly assume high levels of responsibility. It also honors the impulse for growth that is adult, challenges the learner to be totally involved and non-wasteful of this opportunity and non-dependent on the instructor. Group identity starts to form around these notions, and the group is ready to settle down to the actual work before it—as presented in the course outline. The remainder of the morning session is carefully devoted to a fashioning of the foundational properties of making a sound beginning with a student.

After lunch (and the instructor doesn't have to encourage a sense of comraderie, it seems to happen naturally and deepens as the time passes), some review of what has been happening at the School, to each person since graduation and some of the issues that we all face in the field sets the context for the task of socializing another into the field. Here, (as noted earlier) the "reconnection" of supervisors with the school takes place in a serious way. For some this necessitates some review and reminiscence, being bitter, angry, or disappointed, etc. For others, this is a time or re-affirmation of an already good relationship with the School. The discussion is vital because, among other things it deals with ambivalence and brings everyone up to the same starting point, closing some of the discrepancies of feeling and understanding and enabling each to relate to the school as it is in the present, not as it was when they graduated, which may have been from 3 to 10 years ago. This is also a valuable time for dealing with many pragmatic questions that can fuel the anxiety of beginning. While these are rarely serious, they must be dealt with and some common base of understanding which is important to the on-going relationship with the school is established.

The next half day deepens into some serious questions about what supervision means, how it has been conceptualized and some of the models that are espoused in the field. For most, this is a conceptual map that they need to get started, to be filled out by their reading of the text (Kadushin) and other assignments. For most, the tutorial model has greatest familiarity and therefore the approach that they know and will probably use in this first experience. Because the educational function (blended with the administrative function) of supervision is stressed, and the role of the supervisor highly touted as a teaching role, a review of some of the particularly valuable principles of learning are reviewed in a participatory exercise in which each class member is asked to extemporaneously briefly discuss one principle (given them by the instructor) of learning theory (See Kadushin, Chapter 3, for illustrations). This serves to place them in the teacher role and warm them up to the transition from practitioner to teacher. This is an exciting moment, because they see quickly that learning theory is already known to the informal (common-sense terms) yet internalized ways. This confirms their readiness for the new role.

In concluding this first day and one-half of the course, some important things come together. First, a review of some of the high points are covered; second, a kind of "high" i.e., of warm enthusiasm and excitement about embarking on this new venture of professional responsibility is expressed among the group; third; a real support network is nurtured (they are urged to exchange telephone numbers, and to call each other as well as the instructor to share experiences and exchange ideas about problems they encounter; and fourth, each envisions aloud how she will actually begin with her student.

Finally, the assigned readings and paper for the next session are discussed. The realization that they will be expected to write papers brings home the realization that this is school, and that they are again learners facing externally imposed expectations. For most, this sharpens the reality of their involvement as well as their identification with their students and what they will be expecting.

Session II

Having experienced a month in the new role of supervisor in what is perhaps the most anxious time, the supervisors appear for their next all-day session eager to share and exchange ideas about their experiences. A format which positively draws from their common experience has been to move from the idiosyncratic and general in the first hour to the specific by collating and focusing on particular issues in the second hour; and then to move to the practice issues guided by conceptual tools which bring together theory and practice in the final two hours. The final segment is devoted to discussion of papers they have prepared which contain brief illustrations of narrative material from their own work in beginning with their students. These have been received before-hand, duplicated, distributed, and then read during the lunch break. The final segment of this session is devoted to planning for the next months' session, and the assignment of a paper.

The excitement of beginning and sharing with one another is very strong in this session. Most have concentrated on helping their student begin with clients, staff and self, making learning contracts, getting oriented to their field setting and starting to learn their function—all, very basic to performance as an agency representative and learning to a be a social worker. A bit more complex are the subtleties of assessment of "where the student is" in possession of a knowledge-experience base, personal maturity and native skills upon which to build social work skill (e.g., listening, communicating, sensitivity, conceptualizing, values, etc.). Most, at this early stage have started to see their students' learning patterns unfold, e.g., overconcentration on structure and form, staccato questioning rather than listening, becoming engulfed in client problems without a clear focus, inability to partialize, lack of internalization of agency function, etc. Not surprising, most supervisors enjoy the educational function more than the administrative, but already some have had some minor skirmishes with the meaning of authority. The latter is a central theme that seems to run throughout the course. The narrative material affords the opportunity for supervisors to start to look at their own patterns, e.g., of supervising the case rather than the student, of allowing much informal and not enough formal (carefully prepared student agendas and narrative material) supervisory time, including "rapping" rather than supervising, of struggling with how to "transmit" sic, "teach" their own superior knowledge to the student, especially young, inexperienced students, of being over-identified and almost over-eager so that the necessary separation between supervisor and student is sometimes blurred. Most agree that beginning has many components and that at this stage patterns are not established and little depth has been achieved. That is, in fact the next stage. They are asked, in moving to the middle of the semester to keep in mind as they write their papers that time moves quickly and that expectations are such that a deepening and sustaining stage is upon them and that they must "make it happen," i.e., they must teach important concepts, start to expect evidence of learning and application, however clumsy, and they must focus on further development of their own comfort and effectiveness which is then conveyed in their new role.

Session III

The third session is noted by some sobering as supervisors start to experience a deepening relationship with their students; they encounter some resistances and complex learning styles with which they must cope and start to pace themselves for the serious business of teaching and modeling so that the socialization process may go forward.

But for most, by now supervising is becoming a gratifying experience, because having established a foundation most are now enjoying the stage at which their students have seriously connected and have started to take over their own direction. Students have decided that they want to be social workers, and they have started to internalize some theory and in so doing have gained a sense of direction and have a better idea of what they need to learn. As this happens, supervisors can start to feel more secure that they really do know a lot and have something to offer, and that they have created this special relationship; they can, therefore feel secure enough now to confront their own learning problems. At this stage, many sense that they are using their own student (and other) supervisory experience as a model and they start to identify how they wish to individualize their own style so that they will not be carbon copies of others who have influenced them.

Some important issues emerge at this stage. They include: developing a serious degree of comfort with their authority (of knowledge and role) and being able to risk with greater deliberateness and discipline without fear that the relationship will be jeopardized or lost; teaching concepts and principles so that the student may test his new knowledge with clients; reconfirming or modifying earlier educational diagnoses, learning to make available resources for student learning which expand the student's learning base or meet specific educational needs as agreed upon by supervisor and advisor.

There are many idiosyncratic expressions of the supervisory relationship here and these are often the subject of substantial learning. This is the stage at which the rich fabric of the created relationship becomes manifest and there are countless opportunities for special learning to take place based on the complexity of setting and function, personality make-up and style, etc. It is also, as is commonly appreciated, a time when focus may be lost and movement difficult to sustain or even chart. Probably the most important function that the instructor can play at this time is to help these new supervisors stay on course by continuing to clarify with them their professional purpose and the inter-relationship between educational, administrative and supportive functions of supervision.

Session IV

This session has been the official ending of the course with the 5th session devoted to a follow-up. However, this has been modified. More will be said about this later.

The importance of this session is that it marks the time when supervisors have been asked to focus on (write a paper)* reviewing their performance, and identifying their strengths and weaknesses as

---

*This paper is not shared with the class.

a supervisor, the latter to be an agenda for continued work. They have also been asked to come to the session prepared to discuss evaluation of their students. Since this is a short session supervisors work intensively in a task-oriented fashion. First evaluation for students is an urgent experience. It may hold much anxiety, yet it must be regarded as a signal experience because it is a hallmark which conveys so much of the message of the way we in social work think, believe and do. It represents an important part of the ethos of social work, so that it calls for careful handling by the new supervisor.

Evaluation is reviewed as a 5-stage collaborative process with clear prestated boundaries and responsibilities of both supervisor and student (see Kadushin, Chapter V): studying the school's evaluation guide carefully to understand expectations and organize one's self; preliminary supportive and straightforward discussion of steps, purpose, significance, mutual expectations and format are: materials to be used; actual evaluation conference using guide to arrive at an objective appraisal of total functioning, including strengths and weaknesses and areas for future learning; evaluation written and typed to be read and signed by both with the student's right to written addendum; brief review and plan for on-going direction and future learning objectives.

Session V

This session was originally added at the request of the supervisors taking the course who felt the need for a follow-up and exchange. The session has been further modified to include a full discussion of the characteristics of ending. Supervisors have felt that this aided them in "rounding out" the experience by adding specific (textbook) content and direction to students' endings with their clients, the agency and the supervisor herself. Further, it gives the class a chance to return to their support group to share and exchange experiences after an absence of three months. It is not a ritualistic or routine ending, but actually a work session with serious concern about making sound, affirmative endings that will provide firm groundwork for continued learning by their students.

Finally, it provides the supervisors with a final opportunity to talk about their own concerns and to affirm their own work as supervisors.

SUMMARY AND CONCLUSION

The instructional model described here is a blending of an adult educational approach with a short-term sequenced structure. While designed for beginning supervisors who are graduates of the University of Pennsylvania School of Social Work, it could be easily applied to other groups. The approach has been well-received by supervisors and field instruction agencies suggesting that it is on target as a (educational) need-fulfilling, cost-effective approach at a time when the transition from direct practitioner to supervisory roles stirs anxiety and the need for concrete and supportive educational direction.

REFERENCE NOTES

1. Robinson, Virginia P. *The Dynamics of Supervision Under Functional Controls.* University of Pennsylvania Press, Philadelphia, 1949.
2. Arnold, Howard D. and Tybel Bloom. "Institutional Change as a Creative Process: Some Educational and Practice Considerations," *Journal of Social Work Process.* Vol. XIX, 1981, pp. 4-24.
3. Knowles, Malcolm S. *The Adult Learner: A Neglected Species.* Gulf Publishing Company, Houston, 1973.
4. Knowles, Malcolm S. "Innovations in Teaching Styles and Approaches Based Upon Adult Learning," *Education for Social Work.* Spring, 1972, pp. 32-39.
5. Ingalls, John D. *A Trainer's Guide to Andragogy.* Revised Edition, Dept. of HEW, GPO, Washington, D.C.
6. Munson, Carlton E., Editor. *Social Work Supervision: Classic Statements and Critical Issues.* The Free Press, New York, 1979.
7. Kadushin, Alfred. *Supervision in Social Work.* Columbia University Press, New York, 1976.

Achieving Quality Field Instruction in Part-Time Graduate Social Work Programs

Hope W. Davis
Jo Stallings Short
Reginald O. York

ABSTRACT. Due to a growing concern over the non-traditional field arrangements employed in one part-time graduate program, it was decided to empirically test the relative influence upon student learning of structural arrangements, mode of field instruction and the special preparation of the field instructor. A total of 32 students were given the Social Work Practice Problems Test at both the beginning and end of the 1977-78 school year. The results of this study suggest that part-time students as a whole do not gain in practice problem solving ability during field placement. But analysis of the data for sub-groups led to the general conclusion that part-time employed students should have field alternatives that place emphasis upon mode of instruction and the special preparation of the instructor rather than structural arrangements.

Part-time graduate social work education is a challenge to traditional curriculum planning in schools of social work. The additional ingredient of employment among part-time students poses even more reasons for inquiry into the accepted plan of study for graduate social work programs.

The Off-Campus Program at the UNC School of Social Work is one of several non-traditional alternatives to graduate social work education that exists throughout the country. In this program, employed students complete one-half of their MSW degree require-

Hope W. Davis and Jo Stallings Short are part-time instructors in the School of Social Work at the University of North Carolina at Chapel Hill. Reginald O. York is Associate Professor and Director of Field Instruction at the same school.

This paper was presented at the 1979 Annual Program Meeting of the Council on Social Work Education, Boston, Massachusetts (APM Session #35).

45

ments by going to class one day a week for two school years and completing a field placement. Other part-time programs have been developed at the University of Southern California, Virginia Commonwealth University, and Rutgers University to name only a few. While the faculty of these programs express a great deal of confidence in the effectiveness of this alternative in providing education to persons who would not otherwise be able to pursue graduate study,[1] there has been relatively little empirical research regarding the quality of these programs.[2]

Of particular concern to the faculty of these part-time programs have been the non-traditional field arrangements that are necessitated by the constraints of the student's employing agency. In the UNC Off-Campus Program, the employed student can meet the practicum requirement within his own agency or outside of his agency, within a block or concurrent pattern. The field instructor should be a qualified MSW. Typical field arrangements in most schools of social work entail the placement of students with a service, agency, and MSW supervisor that are all new to them. Presumably this newness provides the student with a setting that accentuates the learning objectives and enhances versatility. In the Off-Campus Program, however, not all students are provided a new service in a new agency with a typical field instructor. Due to the constraints and resources of their employing agency, they may remain in their own service area with a new focus on learning and may have their employment supervisor as their field instructor.

As an outgrowth of the above field arrangements, several questions have emerged for the UNC faculty that will be addressed in this paper. The first question to become focused was, "Are there any significant differences in learning for students in typical and atypical field arrangements?" For purposes of this study, "typical" field arrangements are concurrent placements in which students are placed with a service, an agency, and MSW supervisor that are all new to them. Much faculty time and energy had been expended in attempting to create typical field arrangements even though there was little hard evidence that the structural arrangement was the key variable in the student's learning.

Since all of our students had a minimum of two years of paid social work experience, we were also faced with how to meet their individual learning needs when the traditional field practicum objectives were designed for students with no prior social work experience.

Elizabeth Torre has suggested that "students with extensive prior work experience in a helping role may benefit relatively more during the first year from classroom opportunities to acquire the more abstract scientific concepts useful in understanding social work practice in order to provide structures for the growth of their already acquired spontaneous concept."[3] This idea led us to develop an experimental field seminar with four selected students. This seminar met weekly for two semesters and used the experiences of the students to provide the structured content. Process recording was the major teaching tool. The objective was to assist students in conceptualizing their social work practice.

From our experience, we had questioned the impact of structural arrangements upon student learning and had considered mode of instruction a more important variable. This led us to ask, "Is there any significant difference in learning for students experiencing regular process recording (written or audio and video types) and those who do not?" There is no school policy that a field instructor must use process recording as a teaching tool but they are strongly encouraged to use a systematic approach that requires student and field instructor to critically analyze the student's work with clients. A related question about mode of field instruction was, "Are there any significant differences in learning for students whose field instructor participated in the School's Field Instruction Seminar and those who did not?"

The Field Instruction Seminar is offered for all field instructors who are new to the field program. It meets for 10 two-hour sessions during the fall semester. The objective of the Seminar is to acquaint the field instructors with the School's curriculum and assist them in providing a valid educational experience for their students.

The answer to these questions would shed light upon our understanding of the relative utility of field arrangement, mode of field instruction, and the preparation of the field instructor in determining the quality of student learning.

STUDY RESULTS

A total of 32 students in three OCP centers were given the Social Work Practice Problems Test (SWPPT)[4] at both the beginning and end of the 1977–78 school year. Certain circumstances, however, precluded the uniform administration of the test. In the pre-test, students were allowed to take the test home and respond to the questions at their convenience, but the post-test was administered to all students at a single meeting. (It should also be pointed out that the students appeared to be experiencing a high level of anxiety regarding their transfer to the on-campus program at the time of the post-test.)

The pre-test and post-test scores of off-campus program students are displayed in Table 1. Much to the surprise of the authors, the mean score on the post-test (13.96) for these 32 students was lower than their mean score on the pre-test (14.47); however, the difference was not statistically significant (t = −1.08, p > .10). Thus, on the average, the OCP students did not gain in their ability to solve practice problems.

Despite this unexpected decline in scores, it was decided to analyze SWPPT scores among subgroups to determine the association of practice knowledge and the variables identified as being of concern to the education of off-campus students. Of particular concern were the variables of (1) typicality of field arrangement, (2) mode of field instruction, and (3) field instructor preparation. Since the 32 students in this study were educated in three different Off-Campus Centers, it was decided to examine SWPPT scores by center as well.

As with the overall scores, the data for subgroups were analyzed with the use of the paired t test (one-tailed). The results are displayed in Table 2. The only subgroup of students to achieve a gain on SWPPT scores that is worthy of attention was the group of students in one Off-Campus Center whose gain was significant at the .10 level.

Interestingly, however, there were a few subgroups who sustained a significant loss in problem solving ability as measured by the Social Work Practice Problems Test. Of most significance was the discovery that students with field instructors who had not attended the Field Seminar had a significantly lower score on the post-test than pre-test (p < .01). A similar decline was discovered for students with a new service (p < .05), students with block placements (p < .05), and students who had not regularly employed process recording (p < .05). A less significant decline was discovered for students with typical field instructors (p < .10).

As previously mentioned, typical field arrangements for OCP students were concurrent placements in which the students were given a new service (i.e., different from the one for which they had been

TABLE 1

PRE-TEST AND POST-TEST SWPPT SCORES OF OFF-CAMPUS STUDENTS

Student	Pre-Test Score	Post-Test Score	Student	Pre-Test Score	Post-Test Score
1	18	14	17	12	12
2	16	16	18	15	13
3	14	16	19	13	14
4	16	13	20	13	12
5	14	13	21	15	14
6	17	16	22	16	18
7	15	15	23	16	14
8	14	17	24	13	11
9	18	14	25	19	15
10	8	13	26	14	14
11	11	15	27	19	13
12	12	13	28	16	11
13	16	18	29	15	15
14	14	18	30	6	5
15	17	16	31	15	16
16	14	12	32	12	11
			Mean	14.47	13.96

$t = -1.08$, $p > .10$

TABLE 2

SWPPT SCORES OF OCP STUDENTS

Category	Mean Pre-Test	Mean Post-Test	t
1. Center A (N=6)	15.83	14.66	− 1.338, p > .10
2. Center B (N=15)	13.80	14.40	1.62, p < .10
3. Center C (N=11)	14.63	13.00	− 2.176, p < .05
4. Students with Same Service (N=11)	14.27	14.91	1.11, p > .10
5. Students with New Service (N=21)	14.33	13.24	− 1.86, p < .05
6. Students with Typical Field Instructor (N=20)	14.45	13.70	− 1.42, p < .10
7. Students with Atypical Field Instructor (N=12)	14.50	14.42	0.09, p > .10
8. Students in Concurrent Placements (N=17)	14.47	14.47	0.00, p > .10
9. Students in Block Placements (N=15)	14.47	13.40	− 2.08, p < .05
10. Students Who Experienced Regular Process Recording (N=21)	14.23	14.38	0.27, p > .10
11. Students Who Did Not Experience Regular Process Recording (N=11)	14.91	13.18	− 2.11, p < .05
12. Students Whose Field Instructor Had Attended the Field Seminar (N=18)	14.38	14.88	0.82, p > .10
13. Students Whose Field Instructor Had Not Attended the Field Seminar (N=14)	14.57	12.78	− 3.12, p < .01

50

employed to deliver) and were supervised by a person with an MSW degree who was employed as a case supervisor by the field agency. As can be seen by the results of this study, differences in SWPPT scores tend to favor students in the atypical circumstances. To put it more succinctly, students in atypical arrangements were less likely to have suffered a decline in SWPPT scores during field placement.

By comparison, it appears that mode of field instruction and the preparation of the field instructor are more important to student learning than field arrangements. Students whose field instructors were not seminar prepared and students who failed to use process recording had an even more significant decline in scores than students with typical arrangements.

Unexpectedly, it was discovered that SWPPT scores varied by location. Students in one OCP Center had a barely significant gain (p < .10) while those in another center had a significant decline (p < .05). The students in the third center had a non-significant decline.

In summary, the results of this study suggest that OCP students as a whole do not achieve a gain in practice problem solving ability during field placement. But students in atypical arrangements, those who employ process recording, and students with seminar-prepared field instructors are less likely to suffer a loss in ability than students in typical arrangements, students who do not use process recording, and those with field instructors who are not seminar-prepared.

CONCLUSIONS

The findings lead us to explore several tentative conclusions. It may be that the Off-Campus Program is failing to provide adequate field instruction. Although the same objectives are used for the Practica in the OCP as in the regular program and the criteria for selection of field instructors is the same, it is possible that standards are not uniformly adhered to in the OCP. Field learning structures vary considerably. Yet students in non-traditional arrangements tended to do better on the SWPPT than did students in traditional field learning situations.

One might also question the appropriateness of the test. Did it actually measure what was intended? The evidence for reliability and validity documented in the Torre dissertation seems impressive[5] and the instrument had a great deal of face validity to the authors.

It may be that, as Bloom and Farrar have suggested, students in the first year of graduate social work study do not show significant change toward becoming professional social workers. Bloom and Farrar propose that professional development may not be *linear* in nature, progressing in a predictable, continuous fashion through a given curriculum over a two-year time frame. Instead, development may be *spiral,* moving upward but with decided "ups and downs", with shifting concerns in the "foreground" or "background" at any given time in the learning process.[6]

The end of the first year of graduate study may not be a time when consolidation of learning is in the "foreground." Certainly, it is a time of change and insecurity about concluding one field-work experience and beginning another, a time when much student energy is devoted to self-concerns and fear of not measuring up. In the OCP, this is complicated by the fact that students are coping with the demands of moving from the familiar OCP setting to a new campus as well.

Although the items on the SWPPT are related to first-year expectations, one could conceiveably make a case for scheduling the posttest at any number of points in the learning process. In fact, the SWPPT was administered to the same group of students at the completion of the Master's program (May 1979). Only 21 of the original 32 students participated in this latter study. The mean pretest score was 14.86 and the mean posttest was 15.57. The resultant t value of 1.32 was not significant at the .05 level.

Finally, one might reasonably conclude that these students do not significantly gain from traditional field experiences but need a different learning format. Torre and others suggest that students who are accustomed to relying upon past and fairly concrete experiences in making practice judgements, as these students are, may experience pronounced difficulty systematizing these experiences and integrating them with the concepts and models presented in the academic curriculum.[7] We would classify this as a situation in which the new schemata do not fit with the old. This may produce a kind of disequilibrium peculiar to work-experienced students.

Looking at the study findings as a whole, there is the clear suggestion that the mode of field instruction as well as the preparation of the instructor are more significant to improvement of practice judgment than is reliance upon traditional field learning structures. The gains on the SWPPT of students with specially prepared field instructors and students regularly using process recording provide us with clues in regard to the quality and mode of field instruction which can be helpful to these students. The identified difficulty in reorganizing experiences into a new conceptual framework provides a clue to the kind of content emphasis needed.

Building from this, we recommend two models as potential vehicles for field instruction for the part-time, employed student. These are a modified tutorial plan and a seminar/laboratory approach.

In the modified tutorial plan, students, who remain in their employing agencies, pursue individualized learning tasks under the direction of in-agency field instructors who have the MSW. An accompanying seminar for the field instructors, led by full-time faculty, provides a means of facilitating maximum complementarity between class and field. It also provides an on-going opportunity to address major issues and/or difficulties related to the fundamental role switches such arrangements demand of students, field instructors, and other agency staff.

In the seminar/laboratory model, students remain in their regular work assignments and meet in small groups regularly with a faculty member. Content and focus of the seminar is responsive to what the students need to know according to the demands of their immediate practice and in relation to the concepts and principles introduced in the curriculum.[8] Such a model depends heavily upon a developmental approach in terms of both content and group life.[9] Members need to be largely self-directive, working as a team toward mutually determined, specific goals which are commensurate with the stated objectives of the Practica.

An experiment with this model was undertaken with three students in the Charlotte Off-Campus Center during the study year (1977-78). Two of these three students achieved a gain in SWPPT scores while the pre-test and post-test scores for the third were identical; thus, overall these three students did better than any subgroup although the small sample size rendered the gain statistically non-significant ($t = 1.73$, $p > .10$). Nevertheless, the experience was judged by the instructor to have been quite successful.

Process recording can easily and appropriately be employed as a mode of teaching in either model. Both approaches provide maximum and continued opportunity to relate practice to professional theory. Both are responsive to individual needs of students, as the needs come to the "forefront," in a highly individualized way.

On a very practical level, both approaches allow employed students to remain in their own agencies, capitalizing upon their existing knowledge of the agencies. The approaches can be differentially within the same program, depending upon agency and school resources. For example, where agency staff are competent and available, the modified tutorial model may be both feasible and appropriate. Where there are virtually no agency teaching resources, it may be imperative to use the seminar/laboratory model.

In conclusion, the evidence so far suggests we do not have to spend undue energy assuring the prevalence of traditional field arrangements in order to achieve quality field instruction in part-time, graduate social work programs with employed students. There is tentative support for manipulating or adjusting existing models and/or providing innovative approaches, which can be responsive to both the special needs of the students and the particular constraints and resources of school and employing agencies. Two models, the modified tutorial plan and the seminar/laboratory model, have been proposed. Continuing innovation and study is encouraged.

NOTES

1. Five faculty members from part-time programs at Virginia Commonwealth, Rutgers, and the Universities of Southern California, Tennessee, and North Carolina expressed this confidence at a workshop on part-time programs at the 1978 Annual Program meeting of the Council on Social Work Education in New Orleans.

2. Between 1959 and 1974, there was not a single social work doctoral dissertation regarding empirical research into the unique features of part-time programs. There also have been no such studies reported in the *Journal of Education for Social Work* during the past 15 years.

3. Elizabeth L. Torre, "An Exploratory Study of Cognitive Linkage to Prior Experience and the Adult Learner's Problem Solving Abilities: As Observed in the Practicum Component of Graduate Social Work Education," unpublished doctoral dissertation, Tulane University, 1972.

4. *Ibid.* The SWPPT was developed by Elizabeth Torre for use in analyzing the student's ability to solve practice problems typical of those confronted during field placement.

5. *Ibid.*, pp. 86-102. In regard to reliability, both a coefficient of stability and a Spearman-Brown split-half correlation coefficient yielded correlations significant at or beyond .001. All three classifications of validity—criterion-related, content, and construct—appeared to be satisfied.

6. Martin Bloom and Marcella Farrar, "Becoming a Professional Social Worker: Two Conceptual Models," *Social Work Education Reporter*, Vol. 20, No. 2 (April-May, 1972), pp. 23-26.

7. Torre, *op. cit.*, pp. 167-169.

8. Such a model is described in Leonard N. Brown, Daniel Katz, and Theodore Walden, "Student-Centered Teaching: One Analog to Client Centered Practice." *Journal of Education for Social Work*, Vol. 12, No. 3, (Fall, 1976), pp. 11-17.

9. See Emanuel Tropp, "A Developmental Theory," from Robert W. Roberts and Helen Northen, eds., *Theories for Social Work with Groups.* (New York: Columbia University Press, 1976)

An Analysis of Student Perceptions of the Supervisory Conference and Student Developed Agendas for that Conference

Ruth E. Peaper

ABSTRACT. Student perceptions about the value of a supervisory conference were analyzed based on their responses to a 16-item questionnaire. Students were asked to develop agendas of topics they wished to discuss in the supervisory conference. The agendas were studied to determine major areas of discussion planned by students and the type of entries in each category. The questionnaires were re-administered following seven weeks use of the student planned agendas to determine if use of the agendas altered the students' perceived value of the supervisory conference.

The Clinical Supervision model proposed by Cogan (1973) and Goldhammer (1969) for training in Education was later suggested by Anderson (1981) for application in the training of speech-language pathologists. This model consists of a series of phases, one of which is the Supervisory Conference. The Supervisory Conference has been identified as an essential component of the clinical supervision process and serves as a vehicle for ongoing, indepth analysis of client as well as clinician behavior. It is also useful for planning strategies for future clinical sessions. Goldhammer (1969) states that the conference is a time to develop and refine the supervisory contract and to train the teacher in techniques of self supervision.

Ruth E. Peaper, BA, MEd, CCC-SP-L, is Clinic Coordinator, Communication Disorders Clinic, University of Massachusetts, Arnold House, B-6, Amherst, MA 01003.

The author expresses special thanks to the graduate students in speech pathology at the University of Massachusetts who took the time to complete the questionnaires and prepare the weekly agendas.

55

There is some evidence that trainees in speech-language pathology may not perceive the supervisory conference to be of the same
importance in the training process as discussed by proponents of the
Clinical Supervision Model. Culatta, Colucci and Wiggins (1975)
interviewed 18 supervisors and 36 graduate trainees about various
aspects of the supervisory process. A surprising finding was that only 5 of the 36 students interviewed felt the need for regularly
scheduled supervisory conferences. The majority of students indicated a need for conferences only at critical points in the therapy
process or only as needed.

Cogan (1973), Goldhammer (1969), and Michalak (1969) discuss
the importance of preplanning the supervisory conference in order
to assure that the conference is a productive, useful learning experience. In fact, planning the strategy of the conference has been
explained by Cogan and Goldhammer as a distinct phase of the clinical supervision process. These same authors feel that the supervisor
is initially responsible for planning the conference but note that for
later conferences it may be useful for the teacher to take an active
role in the planning process.

The available research about the supervisory conference in
speech-langauge pathology has centered primarily around investigation of verbal interaction patterns and supervisor-supervisee behaviors within the conference (Culatta and Seltzer, 1976, 1977; Irwin,
1975; Roberts and Smith, 1982; and Smith and Anderson, 1982).
To date, there is little information about the planning process that
precedes the supervisory conference and what topics of discussion
are identified in pre-planned conference agendas.

The present investigation focused on the planning process (as
completed by students) for the supervisory conference and the students' view of that conference. The purposes of this study are stated
below.

1. To determine the students' perception of the value of the
   supervisory conference.
2. To analyze student prepared agendas for the supervisory conference.
3. To determine if students who utilized pre-planned agendas
   changed their perceptions about the value of that conference.
4. To determine if the students' perceptions of the value of the
   supervisory conference change as additional clinical experience is obtained.

METHOD

Graduate students in clinical practicum were divided into two groups, experimental and control. A 16-item questionnaire was developed (see Appendix A) about the perceived value of the supervisory conference. The respondents were asked to react to each statement on a 7-point scale with one indicating strong agreement with the statement and seven indicating strong disagreement. In order to allow students time to develop opinions about the supervisory conference, the questionnaires were first completed by students in both groups six weeks into the semester.

Trainees in the experimental group were then asked to develop agendas for the remaining supervisory conferences in the semester. As the purpose was to determine what the students would identify as important areas of discussion, little formal instruction was provided to the students in developing the agendas. Agenda forms were distributed to the experimental group simply listing Client Centered Issues, Clinician Centered Issues and Supervisor Centered Issues with space below each listing (see Appendix B). The students were asked to enter any potential topics of discussion under the appropriate listing. Agendas were planned by students in the experimental group for the remaining seven weeks of the semester.

Finally, the 16-item questionnaire was re-distributed to students in both the experimental and control groups. Students were asked to react to the same statements using the same 7-point rating scale.

SUBJECTS

A total of 21 students (10 in the control group and 11 in the experimental group) completed the initial questionnaire. The trainees were all graduate students currently registered in clinical practicum at one Educational Training Board (ETB) accredited University Training Program. The students were first divided into beginning and advanced level students and were then randomly assigned to the control or experimental group so as to allow for an equal balance of beginning and advanced students in each group.

The second questionnaire was completed by 19 students (10 control and 9 experimental). It was necessary to drop two students from the experimental group because, for various reasons, they were unable to complete the agendas for the full seven weeks.

ANALYSIS OF DATA

The Statistical Package for the Social Sciences (SPSS) (Nie et al., 1975) was used to compute descriptive statistics and make across and within group comparisons. Analyses of variance were completed. A multiple range, a posteriori contrast using the Student-Newman-Keuls procedure was performed when ANOVA was significant ($p < .05$) to determine within group differences.

RESULTS AND DISCUSSION

Responses to Questionnaire

The results of both responses to the questionnaire by the control and experimental groups are given in Table I. As can be noted, there was a significant difference ($p < .05$) in the response to only one statement in the first and second responses to the questionnaire. The experimental group's responses on the second administration of the questionnaire differed from their initial response as they more strongly agreed that they set the tone of the conference (item 11) with means of 1.78 and 3.00 respectively. This result is not surprising as one would expect that utilizing a pre-planned agenda developed by the student would give that student more of an opportunity to control the flow of the meeting.

Although there was some change in the responses to all other statements by the experimental group on their second response to the questionnaire, the change was not great enough to constitute a significant difference. The control group also demonstrated some change in perceptions (although not a significant difference) from the first and second responses on 12 of the 15 statements indicating that perceptions do change slightly with increased experience in the supervisory conference.

As can be noted, most of the initial perceptions by both groups were concentrated at the low end of the 7-point scale. In general, students were in fairly strong agreement that the supervisory conference was useful for the reasons stated on the questionnaire. The lack of significant differences may be explained by the fact that agreement with the statements was fairly strong even on the first response. Therefore, there was little opportunity for a significant change to be measured. Another possible explanation for the lack of change was the duration of the experiment. It is conceivable that seven weeks of using the pre-planned agendas may not be sufficient to produce measurable change.

Item 16 asked the students to estimate the amount of the conference time that is devoted to Client Centered Issues, Clinician Centered Issues and Supervisor Centered Issues. The estimates of the time devoted to each topic area did not change significantly over time and there was no difference between the groups.

Responses to questionnaire items were also analyzed by amount of clinical experience to determine if students' perceptions of the supervisory conference change with additional experience. A significant difference (p < .05) in perceptions was found in the responses to two items and is noted in Table II.

Students with under 100 practicum hours differed from groups with more experience as they did not agree that the weekly conference was useful because the supervisor identifies positive aspects of the clinician's clinical management skills (item 5). Students with under 100 hours differed from those with 201 to 300 practicum hours as they did not agree as strongly that the weekly conference increases confidence in their ability to analyze the performance of the client (item 9). One would expect that if the clinical supervision model is being followed with clinical evaluative skills as a goal for students that they should become more confident in their ability to analyze client performance with additional clinical experience. The results of item 9 appear to confirm this expectation.

Analysis of Agendas

Forty-eight pre-planned agendas were collected and analyzed. A total of 244 entries were made on these agendas over the seven week period. The topics of discussion on the agendas were divided into five major topic areas: Client Performance, Clinician's Performance, Supervisor's Performance, Strategy and Mechanics (usually questions or statements about the operating procedures of the clinic, i.e., due dates for reports, etc.). The percentage of agenda entries in each of the main categories is given in Table III.

Although entries about the supervisor's performance were relatively low (7%), it was found that the distribution of entries, in the other major topic areas did not vary by more than 12%. The percentage of topic items in each major area was also assessed week by week to determine if any shifts in emphasis were apparent over time; however, no clear patterns emerged.

Table I

Responses to Questionnaire

Statement	Control Group		Experimental Group	
	First Response	Second Response	First Response	Second Response
1. The weekly conference is useful in analyzing the performance of my client.	2.10	1.80	1.64	1.55
2. The weekly conference is useful in discussing the adequacy of my cleint's progress.	2.10	2.10	2.18	1.67
3. The weekly conference is useful in developing goals (or revisions of goals) and procedures to meet the needs of my client.	1.40	1.80	1.64	1.89
4. The weekly conference is useful in building my ability to discuss a client on a professional level using succinct, clear language.	3.00	2.50	2.00	1.89
5. The weekly conference is useful because my supervisor identifies positive aspects of my clinical management skills.	3.00	1.90	1.91	1.67
6. The weekly conference is useful because my supervisor identifies aspects of my clinical management skills which should be improved.	2.40	2.10	1.64	1.89
7. The weekly conference is useful because I identify positive aspects of my clinical management skills.	2.80	2.80	2.55	2.22
8. The weekly conference is useful because I identify aspects of my clinical management skills which should be improved.	2.70	2.30	1.82	1.89
9. The weekly conference has increased my confidence in my ability to analyze the performance of my client.	2.30	2.30	2.18	1.78
10. My supervisor is open to topics of discussion I wish to pursue in our conference.	1.90	1.60	1.55	1.44

Table I (continued)

Statement	Control Group First Response	Control Group Second Response	Experimental Group First Response	Experimental Group Second Response
11. I feel that I set the tone of our weekly conference, i.e., I initiate the change in discussion from one topic to another.	2.70	2.40	3.00*	1.78*
12. Participating in the weekly conference gives me the impression that I am an equal team member working to meet the needs of my client.	2.70	2.30	2.90	1.78
13. I feel that my comments regarding the supervisor's input (i.e., suggestions, demonstrations, etc.) are welcome and receive adequate consideration by the supervisor.	2.80	2.10	1.91	1.56
14. I feel my comments regarding the client's performance are welcome and receive adequate consideration from the supervisor.	2.40	1.70	1.45	1.56
15. I feel my comments regarding my performance are welcome and receive adequate consideration from the supervisor.	2.40	2.00	1.64	1.44
16. I feel the discussion in the weekly conference focuses on: (estimate % of conference time devoted to each)				
Client Centered Issues	60.63%	65.00%	56.91%	62.50%
Clinician Centered Issues	24.38%	28.89%	24.64%	26.25%
Supervisor Centered Issues	15.00%	7.22%	18.27%	11.25%

*indicates significant difference between responses

1 = Strongly Agree ⟶ 7 = Strongly Disagree

Table II

Significant Difference in Perceptions by Number of Practicum Hours

Statement	Under 100 Practicum Hours	101-200 Practicum Hours	201-300 Practicum Hours	Over 300 Practicum Hours
5. The weekly conference is useful because my supervisor identifies positive aspects of my clinical management skills.	4.00_a	2.00_b	1.55_b	1.38_b
9. The weekly conference has increased my confidence in my own ability to analyze the performance of my client.	3.29_a	2.12_{ab}	1.55_b	1.87_{ab}

Note: Multiple range tests using the Student-Newman-Keuls procedure were performed when ANOVA was significant ($p < .05$). The subscripts designate those groups which were found to be significantly different using the above procedure. Means in each row with different subscripts are significantly different from one another. ab indicates this group was not significantly different from the other groups.

Table III

Percentage of Total Agenda Items in Each Category

	Number of Entries	Percentage
Evaluation of Client's Performance	73	29.9
Evaluation of Clinician's Performance	55	22.5
Evaluation of Supervisor's Performance	17	7.0
Strategy	43	17.6
Mechanics	56	23.0

The agendas were further analyzed to determine what types of entries were made in each of the major categories. Entries in each category were placed in one of the following classifications.

1. Positive Evaluation of Performance or Strategy
2. Negative Evaluation of Performance or Strategy
3. Question (Entries that may have been about the performance or strategy but that were recorded in question form i.e., "Am I utilizing verbal reinforcements adequately?"
4. Statement—any observation made that was in declarative form but did not imply positive or negative evaluation. Some entries were fairly cryptic and it could not be determined if a positive or negative evaluation was implied.

The results of this analysis are explained in Table IV.

Some interesting trends emerged from this analysis. It was found that students made a much higher percentage of positive evaluations about the supervisor's performance (88.2%) than they did about the client (26%) or themselves (21.8). They apparently did not feel comfortable making any negative evaluation of the supervisor's performance (at least on these agendas) as no entries were found in that category for the supervisors. Negative Evaluations about the client's performance totaled 13.7% and about their own performance were 12.7%.

Previous research about the supervisory conference has found that very little conference time is devoted to evaluation. Culatta and Seltzer (1976) studied 12 weeks of supervisory conferences and found that only 9% of the responses were evaluative in nature with two-thirds of the evaluation statements made by the supervisor.

Table IV

Analysis of Agenda Entries in Each Major Category

	Evaluation of Client's Performance	Evaluation of Clinician's Performance	Evaluation of Supervisor's Performance	Strategy	Mechanics
Positive Evaluation	26%	21.8%	88.2%	0%	0%
Negative Evaluation	13.7%	12.7%	0%	2.3%	0%
Question	11%	43.6%	5.9%	39.5%	26.8%
Statement	49.3%	21.8%	5.9%	58.1%	73.2%

Roberts and Smith (1982) studied supervisory conferences over a six week period and found that conferences were more analytic than evaluative. The total number of evaluative entries (positive and negative) was computed and found to be 49 or 20% of the total items listed on the agendas. In addition, many of the entries that were presented as questions should have prompted some sort of evaluative discussion (i.e., "Is my rate too fast?"). Thirty-five or 14% of the total entries listed were in this category. When these two categories are combined, a total of 34% of the entries were evaluative in nature. It appears that at least when planning the conference, students do consider evaluative discussion to be important as over one-third of the entries were in that category. The actual conferences were not analyzed in this study so it can not be determined if the amount of actual evaluative conference responses would exceed the 9% found by Culatta and Seltzer (1976).

The amount of entries in question form also produced interesting results particularly in the high percentage (43.6%) of questions entered about clinicians performance and about strategy (39.5%). It appears that students are much more likely to make a declarative statement or evaluation about a client or supervisor's performance but phrase entries about their own performance ("Did I reinforce consistently and accurately?") and strategy ("Would relaxation exercises be useful?") in question form. While there was no real change in the distribution of major topic areas over time, there was a distinct reduction in the amount of questioning entries over time. Fifty-eight percent of the question entries for evaluation of Clinician's Performance were found in agendas from Weeks One and Two. Only 12.5 of the questioning entries in that same category were found in agendas from Weeks Six and Seven. In the Strategy Category 47.1% of the question entries were in the first two weeks and 11.7% in the last two weeks. These results indicate that students apparently become more confident in their own evaluative skills over time (at least on paper) as fewer entries are in question form.

SUMMARY

The results of the present investigation indicate that in general, students do agree that the conference is useful for evaluation of client and clinician performance and in developing goals and procedures to meet the client's need. Students who utilized the pre-planned agendas agreed more strongly that they set the tone of the weekly conferences. Students with under 100 practicum hours differed from groups with more experience as they did not agree as strongly that conferences were useful because the supervisor identifies positive aspects of their clinical management skills or that the conference increased their confidence in their ability to analyze the client's performance.

Analysis of agenda entries found that the distribution of entries in major categories did not change over time. However, the number of questioning entries in Evaluation of the Clinician's Performance and in Strategy showed a definite decline over time. Over one-third of the entries were evaluative in nature.

These results pose some intriguing questions for further investigation.

1. Do the entries on the student pre-planned agenda reflect the actual topics of discussion in the conference and with a similar distribution.
2. If over one-third of agenda entries are evaluative in nature why did a previous study find that only 9% of actual conference responses were in this category.
3. Would agendas planned by the supervisor consist of similar topics and distribution.

There is certainly need for additional research in the area of supervisory conferences. It would appear that this research should also consider the planning phase which precedes the actual conference. It is conceivable that at least some actual conference behavior, the amount of supervisor/supervisee talk time, percentage of evaluative statements, control of the session, may be altered with the use of a pre-planned agenda.

BIBLIOGRAPHY

Anderson, J. Training of supervisors in speech-language pathology and audiology. *Asha,* 1981, 23, 77-82.
Cogan, M. *Clinical Supervision.* Boston: Houghton Mifflin, 1973.
Culatta, R., and Seltzer, H. Content and sequence analysis of the supervisory session. *Asha,* 1976, 18, 8-12.
Culatta, R., and Seltzer, H. Content and sequence analysis of the supervisory session: A report of clinical use. *Asha,* 1977, 19, 523-526.

Culatta, R., Colucci, S., and Wiggins, E. Clinical supervisors and trainees: Two views of a process. *Asha*, 1975, 17, 152-157.

Goldhammer, R. *Clinical Supervision.* New York: Holt, Rinehart and Winston, 1969.

Irwin, R. Verbal behaviors of supervisors and speech clinicians during micro-counseling. *Central States Speech Journal*, 1975, 26, 45-51.

Michalak, D. Supervisory conferences improve teaching. *Research Bulletin*, 1969, 5.

Nie, H.H., Hull, C.H., Jenkins, J.G., Steinbrenner, K., & Bent, D.H. Statistical Package for the Social Sciences. New York: McGraw-Hill Book Company, 1975.

Roberts, J.E., and Smith, K.S. Supervisor-supervisee role differences and consistency of behavior in supervisory conferences. *Journal of Speech and Hearing Research*, 1982, 25, 428-434.

Smith, K., and Anderson, J. The relationship of perceived effectiveness to verbal interaction/content variables in supervisory conferences in speech-language pathology. *Journal of Speech and Hearing Research*, 1982, 25, 252-261.

APPENDIX A

Instructions
Please Read Carefully

The following are statements about the weekly conference with your clinical supervisor. Please indicate on the scale how strongly you agree or disagree with each statement. Use the end spaces of the scale to indicate that you *strongly* agree or *strongly* disagree, and the middle space to indicate that you neither agree or disagree. There are no right or wrong answers, I am simply interested in your perceptions about each of the statements based on *your* experience in the weekly conference. Please check your approximate number of clinical hours to date on the lines below and then complete the questionnaire. Thank you.

——under 100 clinical hours   ——201-300 clinical hours
——101-200 clinical hours   ——over 300 clinical hours

1. The weekly conference is useful in analyzing the performance of my client.

   Strongly Agree—— —— —— —— ——Strongly Disagree

2. The weekly conference is useful in discussing the adequacy of my clients progress.

   Agree—— —— —— —— —— ——Disagree

3. The weekly conference is useful in developing goals (or revisions of goals) and procedures to meet the needs of my client.

   Agree—— —— —— —— —— —— ——Disagree

4. The weekly conference is useful in building my ability to discuss a client on a professional level using succinct, clear language.

   Agree—— —— —— —— —— —— ——Disagree

5. The weekly conference is useful because my supervisor identifies positive aspects of my clinical management skills.

   Agree—— —— —— —— —— —— ——Disagree

6. The weekly conference is useful because my supervisor identifies aspects of my clinical management skills which should be improved.

   Agree—— —— —— —— —— —— ——Disagree

7. The weekly conference is useful because I identify positive aspects of my clinical management skills.

   Agree—— —— —— —— —— —— ——Disagree

8. The weekly conference is useful because I identify aspects of my clinical management skills which should be improved.

   Agree—— —— —— —— —— —— ——Disagree

9. The weekly conference has increased my confidence in my own ability to analyze the performance of my client.

   Agree—— —— —— —— —— —— ——Disagree

10. My supervisor is open to topics of discussion I wish to pursue in our conference.

    Agree—— —— —— —— —— —— ——Disagree

11. I feel that I set the tone of our weekly conferences, i.e., I initiate the change in discussion from one topic to another.

    Agree—— —— —— —— —— —— ——Disagree

12. Participating in the weekly conferences gives me the impression that I am an equal team member working to meet the needs of my client.

    Agree—— —— —— —— —— —— ——Disagree

13. I feel that my comments regarding the supervisors input (i.e., suggestions, demonstrations, etc) are welcome and receive adequate consideration by the supervisor.

Agree— — — — — — —Disagree

14. I feel my comments regarding the clients performance are welcome and receive adequate consideration from the supervisor.

Agree— — — — — — —Disagree

15. I feel my comments regarding my performance are welcome and receive adequate consideration from the supervisor.

Agree— — — — — — —Disagree

16. I feel the discussion in the weekly conference focuses on: (estimate % of conference time devoted to each)
Client centered issues——
Clinician centered issues——
Supervisor centered issues——

APPENDIX B

Agenda for Weekly Conference   Week of ———

Client/Clinician ——————————— Supervisor ———

Client-Centered Issues:

Clinician-Centered Issues:

Supervisor-Centered Issues:

Mentor-Mentee Match
in Training Programs
Based on Chickering's Vectors
of Development

Ann M. Orzek

While the concept of mentoring originated in Homer's Odyssey, it has only been recently that the importance of a mentoring relationship early in adulthood has been discussed. To truly understand the reason for the importance of this process, the multiplicity of the roles of the mentor must be considered. O'Neil and Wrightsman (in press) explain that mentoring "exists when a professional person serves as a resource, sponsor, and transitional figure for another person (usually, but not necessarily, younger) who is entering the profession." The mentor represents values, skills, and success that the mentee (person being mentored) wishes to acquire, and provides knowledge, advice, challenge, and support. Levinson, Darrow, Klein, Levinson, and McKee (1978) in their definition emphasize the "transitional figure" role of the mentor, i.e., representing both parent and peer, who helps the mentee move from child to adult. It includes teaching, sponsoring, hosting, and guiding. These definitions, therefore, consider both the professional and personal development of the mentee. While neither of these definitions specifically indicates the mentor-mentee relationship need occur within an academic environment, Lester and Johnson (1981) include in their definition that "mentoring as a function of educational institutions can be defined as a one-to-one learning relationship between an older person and younger person based on modeling behavior and extended dialogue." They emphasize that the mentoring pro-

Ann M. Orzek is a Doctoral Candidate in Counseling Psychology, The University of Kansas, Lawrence, KS 66044.

cess is a way of individualizing a person's education by allowing connection "with a college staff member who is experienced in a field or specific set of skills."

The essence of these perspectives is that the mentor-mentee relationship is (a) between individuals with different levels of expertise, (b) much broader than mere instruction or supervision, and (c) reinforcing in some way for each. The mere existence of these characteristics within a relationship, however, does not necessarily indicate that a mentoring relationship is in progress. While O'Neil and Wrightsman (in press) compiled a list of the role functions and role definitions of mentoring, not all will be present in each mentoring relationship or for each mentor. Different functions and roles of the mentor may be elicited by different mentees. The question, therefore, is whether the characteristics of the mentee determine which role and function of the mentor is exhibited or does the mentor seek certain mentees which allow for the functions the mentor finds most comfortable? What this suggests in either case is that the sine qua non of a mentoring relationship is a match between the characteristics of the mentor and the mentee both in terms of needs and what can be provided by each.

While individual differences are obviously present, the needs of the mentee may be determined, at least partially, by the particular state of development he or she is in. The purpose of this paper, therefore, is to propose a model of mentoring based on match between the particular stage of development of the mentee and the functions valued by the mentor. While this is not to suggest that the mentor's functioning remain constant, i.e., does not vary as a function of his/her own development, the focus will be on the mentee's needs as determined by the particular stage of the professional and personal development. By the determination of certain needs of the mentee, the matching to a particular mentor based on functions she or he is able to provide will allow for a more fruitful relationship for both members. Implications for training programs will then be discussed.

BACKGROUND

While a "mentee" can be of any chronological age, the time designated to secure a "first" mentor relationship is early adulthood. Levinson et al. (1978) state that the ages from 17 to 22 are when young adults enhance their development through a mentoring relationship. Sheehy (1977) supports this by concluding that one of the tasks of the Trying Twenties is to find a mentor if possible. It would seem most reasonable, therefore, to look to a theory of development for this particular age group. Arthur Chickering (1969) has identified seven vectors of development for young adults: achieving competence, managing emotions, becoming autonomous, establishing identity, freeing interpersonal relationships, clarifying purpose, and developing integrity. These areas are called "vectors" because each seems to have magnitude and direction. For each potential mentee, therefore, different vectors may determine the characteristics desired in a mentor. By exploring the essence of each vector, the function of the mentor which best allows for the progression through the stage can be established.

Achieving Competence. Although Chickering describes three types of competence, the essence of this vector is that the mentee has a sense of competence: "the confidence one has in his ability to cope with what comes and to achieve successfully what he sets out to do" (Chickering, 1969). This confidence can be the result of past experiences. In establishing social and interpersonal competence, the mentee may seek from the mentor a close, personal relationship. Flaningam and Jenkins (1983) report that in their study of 200 freshmen and seniors in an introductory interpersonal communications course, potential mentees were more likely to view a mentoring relationship as an interpersonal one rather than a professional one. Their expectations were that mentors were persons with whom to have a close relationship, and professional status is of little importance in the role of the mentor. This corresponds to the contention of Phillips-Jones (Flaningam, 1983) that the "first" ingredient for the successful mentor-mentee relationship is a good interpersonal relationship. This would suggest that both mentor and mentee need to be capable of intimacy. Since one of the tasks of the Trying Twenties (Sheehy, 1977) is to form the capacity for intimacy, it would seem reasonable that the mentee should be able to find a mentor who provides the stimulus to expand on the completion of this task. The specific role functions summarized by O'Neil and Wrightsman (in press) which could facilitate this process include believing in the mentee, helping the mentee define his/her newly emerging self, listening without distorting, acting as a sounding board, reflecting feelings, and helping clarify the mentee's values.

A second type of competence which the potential mentee is trying to develop is intellectual competence. The mentor can act to stimulate ideas, give information, provide opportunities to learn, enlarge the mentee's perspective, have an awareness of the teachable moment and use it, and assess the state of the mentee's knowledge (O'Neil & Wrightsman, in press).

Managing emotions. Emotions need to be experienced and recognized. The two basic impulses to manage are aggression and sex. The potential mentee will need to be aware of prioritizing between sexual/romantic feelings and career issues at certain points in their lives. The mentor can help the mentee set goals for life and career and discuss and clarify with the mentee personal-professional dreams and reflect feelings. In working with the mentee to manage aggression, the mentor can help the mentee fight inner battles, conquer inner fears, doubts, and obstacles (O'Neil & Wrightsman, in press).

Becoming autonomous. The potential mentee will need to develop both emotional and instrumental independence. As the mentee becomes more emotionally independent, there is less need for reassurance. This can be accomplished by the mentor believing in the mentee. As instrumental independence increases, the mentee can cope with problems without seeking help. The mentor may need to relinquish direct guidance and instead identify resources for the mentee's learning and growth (O'Neil & Wrightsman, in press).

Establishing identity. Development of identity depends in part upon the other vectors already mentioned: competence, emotions, and autonomy. It may include personal and professional identity. For the development of professional identity, the mentor may be "opening doors" for the mentee and help define the newly emerging self. In Flaningam's study, however, the respondents stated that professional qualities are not considered to be important in the mentor. What may be more important, therefore, is the modeling of the "process" of being a professional and not the outcome. The mentor may need to reinforce the learning of the profession and not the performance within (O'Neil & Wrightsman, in press).

Freeing personal relationships. This vector is concerned with developing tolerance for a wider range of persons. In essence, this would include the mentor acting as a sounding board and modeling tolerance for the mentee's perspective and helping to enlarge it.

Clarifying purpose. Development of purpose requires formulating plans and priorities that integrate avocational, vocational, and life style plans. The mentor can help set goals for life and career, help in decision-making, and help the mentee act on the decision (O'Neil & Wrightsman, in press). *Developing integrity.* The prospective mentee needs to clarify beliefs which will provide a guide for behavior. Within this framework, values are identified and acted upon. According to O'Neil and Wrightsman, the mentor can help identify the mentee's values both personally and professionally, and discuss their ramifications.

IMPLICATION FOR TRAINING

Chickering's seven vectors of development and the functions of the mentor which provide interpersonal stimulation for each have been described. The issue remains, however, that not all potential mentees will manifest each vector in the same direction or magnitude, and not all prospective mentors will exhibit all 25 identified functions. How then can the possibility of optimal match be increased?

O'Neil and Wrightsman (in press) list recommendations concerning issues to be discussed once the mentor-mentee relationship is established, but little has been written concerning the process of initial match early in the mentee's training. As in most areas in which a dearth of research exists, it is common to borrow from the models of processes in which common functions exist. One role of the mentor may be that of supervisor. The supervision model of Loganbill, Hardy, and Delworth (1982) provides a developmental sequence through which the supervisee proceeds. The three stage model of Loganbill et al. (1982) defines Stagnation as the first stage followed by Confusion and Integration. If the potential mentee is a neophyte in his/her professional training in psychology, it may be assumed there would be some parallels between the potential mentee and beginning supervisee and therefore they may share some of the same characteristics. In describing the Stagnation stage, Loganbill et al. (1982) use "unawareness" as a primary indicator with dualistic thinking existing in parallel. The supervisees in this stage will view the world with a narrow and rigid perspective. They will deny their own power and rely heavily on the expertise of the supervisor. From this model, therefore, it could be concluded that the mentor, while ostensibly matching functions with vectors of a particular mentee, may not in actuality be a good choice because the manner in which the functions are delivered may not take their level of development into consideration. Therefore, in the possible matching of mentor and mentee in training programs, the following issues need to be considered:

1. Developmental tasks (vectors) currently being worked through by the mentee.
2. Functions to be performed by the mentor.
3. Cognizance on both parts of the specific needs manifested in the Stagnation stage of development.

These can be discovered by:

1. Graduate students discussing among themselves different factors (tasks) influencing their development.
2. Faculty discussing which functions they most enjoy performing.
3. More communication between potential mentees and mentors both formally (seminars, classes, presentations) and informally (office visits, meetings in lounges etc.) to compare the interests of each group.

FURTHER QUESTIONS

This paper has merely begun to consider the factors which will enhance the match between potential mentees and mentors. It has concentrated specifically on potential mentees who are entering a professional training program and issues that they face because of their level of development. Further questions to be investigated would include:

1. What are the specific issues to be dealt with by mentees at a later stage of development?
2. Are there specific stages of development mentors experience in their role as mentor?
3. What are the problems faced when the match between mentor and mentee becomes dysfunctional due to increased development of each?
4. Is there a particular set of characteristics which dictate the inability for someone to mentor? to be mentored?

SUMMARY

By the use of Chickering's vectors of development, specific issues for potential mentees were identified. These were then matched with specific functions of mentors. Parallels were drawn to the supervision model of Loganbill et al. (1982) as to the specific attitudes of the supervisee in the Stagnation stage. Implications for training programs were discussed as were questions which deal with expansion of certain parts of the model.

REFERENCES

Burton, A. The mentoring dynamic in therapeutic transformations. *The American Journal of Psychoanalysis*, 1977, *37*, 115-122.

Chickering, A. W. *Education and identity.* San Francisco: Jossey-Bass, 1969.

DeCoster, D. A., & Brown, R. D. Mentoring relationships and the educational process. In R. D. Brown & D. A. DeCoster (Eds.), *New Directions for Student Services: Mentoring-Transcript Systems for Promoting Student Growth*, No. 19. San Francisco: Jossey-Bass, 1982.

Flaningam, R. R., & Jenkins, V. Y. An investigation of the interpersonal aspects of the mentor-protege relationship. Presented at the Association for Women in Psychology Convention, Seattle, 1983.

Lester, V., & Johnson, C. The learning dialogue: Mentoring. In J. Fried (Ed.), *New Directions for Student Services: Education for Student Development*, No. 15. San Francisco: Jossey-Bass, 1981.

Levinson, D. J., Darrow, C. L. Klein, E. B., Levinson, M. H., & McKee, B. *The season's of a man's life.* New York: Alfred A. Knopf, 1978.

Loganbill, C. R., Hardy, E. V., & Delworth, U. Supervision: A conceptual model. *The Counseling Psychologist*, 1982, *10*(1). (Monograph)

O'Neil, J. M., & Wrightsman, L. S. The mentoring relationship in psychology training programs. In G. F. Sumper & S. Walfish (Eds.), *Clinical, counseling, and community psychology: A student guide to graduate training and professional practice.* Irvington Publishers, in press.

Sheehy, G. *Passages.* New York: Bantam Books, 1977.

BOOK REVIEWS

FIELD INSTRUCTION: TECHNIQUES FOR SUPERVISORS, by Suanna J. Wilson. *The Free Press, New York, 1981, $27.95, 348 pp.*

Wilson writes a self-instructional manual for agency-based field instructors in social work education. She presents procedures and techniques to structure and provide educational supervision to BSW and MSW students during their field placements and attends peripherally to field instruction issues most pertinent to school faculty, agency administrators, and students.

The book's organization generally follows the field instruction placement process. It prefaces with a strong statement of the author's biases and a chapter which describes characteristics of social work education, field instruction, and accreditation. In this section she promises a comprehensive rendering of her highly structured approach to field instruction and sharply criticizes social work education for producing too many mediocre professionals. The remainder of the book delivers on her promise. She deals completely with her own field instruction approach—not once mentioning any alternative models. Her critical comments are certainly worth some attention in social work education. However, they reflect a disturbing pattern that runs throughout the book—documentation of strongly stated criticisms only through the author's own personal experience and a pedantic, almost arrogant, tone. Nevertheless, the author seems genuinely concerned with the quality of professional social work practice and much of her approach would increase the quality of students' field learning.

The approach itself is presented in Chapters 2 through 12. The earlier chapters discuss criteria for selecting field placements and instructor/supervisors, the use of the preplacement interview, and common anxieties of students and (too often neglected in the literature) the supervisors. Following chapters list the complementary roles and responsibilities of the school and agency in orienting students to the field placement and the central field instruction process of assigning learning experiences, teaching competencies, and monitoring and assessing the student's performance. The uses of an educational contract and structured process recording are especially recommended and detailed through examples. The chapters on the educational contract (Chapter 6), process recording (Chapter 9), and guidelines for writing performance evaluations (Chapter 11) are the strongest in the book in their contribution to practical tools for the new and experienced field instructor and their potential benefit for the student. The presented formats fruitfully could be adapted to any supervisory processes for professional development purposes.

The book concludes with two special chapters—one on the evaluation of the unsatisfactory student and one on the legal aspects of field instruction. The latter presents a prototype of an agency-school contract and deals with such legal issues as grievance hearings, lawsuits, and confidentiality. Then, the author includes an 8-section, 100-page appendix with (among other material) critical incidents of problem situations for field instructors, consultants, supervisors, and trainers of field instructors; individual and group training exercises for writing performance evaluations and using the author's analytical thinking model for casework and recording; outlines and forms for assessing field learning experiences by field instructors and students; and a list of ingredients for a comprehensive field instructional program which the author suggests could be useful in planning the content of a field instructional manual. The appendix material contributes documents which could readily be adapted to agencies and/or schools with developing field instruction programs and could serve as models against which established programs could compare and refine their written manuals and forms. This section also reflects another quirk of the author's found throughout the book—her proclivity for lists, e.g., 22-item checklist for school's and 25-item list for agency's orientation of student to field, 53-item checklist for the field instructor's assignment of learning experiences, 26-item list of criteria for assigning cases, 32-item checklist for determining student's level of interviewing skills, 19-item list of characteristics of well-written versus poorly written performance evaluations, and a list of 21 ingredients of a comprehensive field instruction program.

With ten years of experience as a field instructor for BSW and

MSW students and additional experience as a field work coordinator and program director in social work education, this reviewer finds Wilson's book loaded with familiar examples and yet too one-sided. Especially the new field instructor will find much direction in this work for what to do to develop the student's professional skills on the job but little to ensure that this learning is part of an overall instructional design. The tools for the effective field instructor, such as those Wilson presents, must flow from the purpose of field instruction in the educational program. If the purpose of field instruction is integrating knowledge, value, and skill learning in practice competencies, then programs of social work education in conjunction with field instructors need to be clear about the breadth and depth of specified competency objectives and use these as tools in instructional designs which can build bridges to competence for the student. This task requires field instructors to demand and use more direction from the school and schools to be more rigorous in their stated instructional outcomes and more planful in their use of field experiences (early observations, simulations, graduated course-related placements, classroom-based field projects, and internships) than Wilson's book suggests. Attention to the field instructor's part in instructional designs for field learning would promote field instruction more as an internship for a profession rather than an apprenticeship for a trade. Without this direction in instructional design, the field instructor using Wilson's pragmatic techniques, even with the best of intents, may influence learning more characteristic of the latter than the former. Wilson paints a detailed model of the ideal field instructor as a professional supervisor, but this seems only half the picture. The other half must place the field instructor at that pivotal point in the instructional process as an educator who in partnership with the school enables the student to achieve the *school's* objectives of a beginning or advanced professional social worker.

Joseph D. Anderson
Professor and Chairperson
Department of Social Work
Shippensburg University
Shippensburg, PA

QUALITY FIELD INSTRUCTION IN SOCIAL WORK: PRO-
GRAM DEVELOPMENT AND MAINTENANCE. Edited by
Bradford W. Sheafor and Lowell E. Jenkins. *New York: Longman
Inc., 1982. 290 pp. $25.00 cloth, $15.95 paper.*

This volume is composed of fifteen chapters which are presented
in five parts with an appendix in the form of a nineteen page annotated bibliography. Part I contains three chapters which address the
context in which field instruction occurs, the big picture, i.e., an
overview, history of field instruction and the use of learning theory.
Part II contains two chapters which address curriculum issues, one
addresses field learning objectives and the second addresses field-
related evaluation issues. Part III contains five chapters which address the rights and responsibilities of the key figures in field instruction which includes the school administrator, the field director
or coordinator, the placement agency, the student and the client.
Part IV contains four chapters which present content on field
instruction process, structure, methods and integration of class and
field learning. Part V is composed of one chapter which presents
case material to illustrate examples of practice tasks, educational
content, and student learning tasks at each stage of the problem-
solving process, i.e., engagement, assessment and planning, intervention, evaluation, and termination.

The title of the book suggests that its content is aimed primarily to
those who are or hope to be engaged in social work field instruction,
which includes current social work practitioners, school and agency
administrators, and present and future social work educators at the
undergraduate and graduate level in either school or agency settings.

The content is organized around nine themes: (1) the legitimacy
of field instruction; (2) the field instructor role of teacher as opposed
to supervisor; (3) the uniqueness of the field experience for individual learning; (4) the importance of clearly stated learning objectives;
(5) the importance of coordination efforts to minimize communication problems between the various field instruction actors, i.e.,
school, agency, field instructor, student and client; (6) the in-
dividuality of each school field programs; (7) the applicability of
basic field instruction principles across levels of instruction BSW-
MSW, practice setting, or geographical area; (8) recognition of the
art quality of field instruction and the commitment to utilize knowledge of teaching methods and learning processes; and (9) the accep-

tance of the challenge to upgrade the standing of field instruction to assure academic credibility.

The editors and contributors of this volume have performed a significant contribution in bringing together this collection of articles that well represent the major concerns of social work educators and practitioners engaged in field instruction directly or indirectly. The inclusion of units addressing the rights and responsibilities of the student and the client as actors in the field instruction gestalt attests to the thoroughness with which the subject matter is considered. Although all chapters included relevant content that would interest readers engaged in some form of field supervision, a number of chapters deserve special mention because of their superior quality such as Sheafor and Jenkin's initial chapter which gives the reader an overview of the subject and presents three approaches to field instruction: the apprenticeship orientation, the academic approach, and the articulated approach; the Aase George chapter which describes the history of social work field instruction; the Pilcher and Brennen chapters which address the questions of field learning objectives and evaluation issues; the Siporin chapter by Dea, Grist, and Myli which provides a case to illustrate how a field instructor may relate case material to the learning tasks at the various stages of the intervention process. Space does not permit elaborating on other strong features of the text such as the excellent preface to each part of the book and the attention given to consistency in the use of key terms.

The narrow focus of the content is both a strength and a weakness. On the positive side the narrow focus permitted the authors to examine this one area of social work education in-depth. On the negative side, the narrow perspective did not permit comparison with similar efforts in related fields such as in psychology, psychiatry, psychiatric nursing and other disciplines that make use of supervised practice learning. Another scope issue which presents room for debate is the issue of breadth given to the membership or actors included as responsible parties in the gestalt of field instruction, i.e., program directors, field coordinators, placement agency, student, and client. On the abstract level the inclusion of student and client is an exciting idea which is in keeping with the profession's ethical principles and in reality all these actors influence outcomes of field instruction. On an operational level, one needs to acknowledge differences in knowledge power which make the actors unequal, the student and client are highly dependent on the school and the agency actors for guidance and quality control. The rights of students and clients certainly must be respected. Students need to be protected from choosing alternatives that are not in keeping with their educational needs. The average student chooses the path of least resistance which may lead to long term negative consequences. Randolph raises some important questions with regard to client's rights that need further consideration by the profession. As Randolph indicates, aside from agreeing to be seen by a student, it is difficult to conceive how a client could be held responsible for some responsibility in the student's education.

Overall the book follows its title theme, for it addresses all the major issues that affect quality field instruction and shows how case material can be used in field instruction. The text is uneven with regard to source documentation, three chapters include no references. The annotated bibliography includes many fine sources in the 108 citations listed, the major criticism is that the works cited are for the most part dated, only five are recent 1980 listings.

In summary, this volume makes an important contribution to one dimension of supervision, student field instruction. After reading this volume, the reader will have a comprehensive picture of the various dimensions of social work education which includes the field component. The gestalt of field instruction is presented by examining the roles and responsibilities of its actors, their interdependence in bringing out a successful program which produces a competent practitioner. The editors and contributors are to be commended for this well presented volume.

Herman Curiel
Assistant Professor
School of Social Work
University of Oklahoma